Grade 2

Addison-Wesley Mathematics

Building Thinking Skills Workbook

▲▼ Addison-Wesley Publishing Company

Menlo Park, California ■ *Reading, Massachusetts* ■ *New York*
Don Mills, Ontario ■ *Wokingham, England* ■ *Amsterdam* ■ *Bonn*
Sydney ■ *Singapore* ■ *Tokyo* ■ *Madrid* ■ *San Juan*

ISBN 0-201-27219-9

ABCDEFGHIJK-HC-943210

Table of Contents

Framed Numbers

Match the clue to the 10-frame pictures.
Count on or back to solve.

1. 1 more than 13

2. 3 less than 8

3. 2 more than 7

4. 4 less than 20

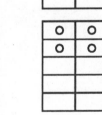

Write your own clues.
Draw counters on the 10-frames.

5. ____ more than ____

6. ____ less than ____

Name _____

Going Shopping

A 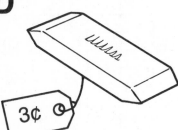 5¢

B 6¢

C 7¢ 1¢

D 3¢

E  4¢

F 2¢

G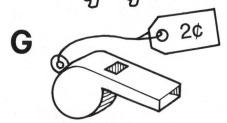

Which two did the person buy?

1. Lee spent 8¢.

He bought I **B** and I ̶G̶.

2. Lana spent 5¢.

She bought I **E** and I ___.

---

3. Tom spent 7¢.

He bought I **B** and I ___.

4. Pam spent 4¢.

She bought I **F** and I ___.

---

5. Sue spent 6¢.

She bought I **G** and I ___.

6. Ted spent 8¢.

He bought I **D** and I ___.

Name _____

Leaving the Cage

How many flew away?

1. Start with 8.

7 flew away.

2. Start with 6.

_____ flew away.

3. Start with 5.

_____ flew away.

4. Start with 7.

_____ flew away.

5. Start with 6.

_____ flew away.

6. Start with 7.

_____ flew away.

The Sleepover Party

Read the story.
Look at the picture.
Write a number sentence
to answer each question.

Nan and Fran are twins.
They invited some friends to sleep over.

1. How many friends did they invite?

_____ ◯ _____ ☐ _____

Six girls at the party have stuffed animals.

2. How many are teddy bears?

_____ ◯ _____ ☐ _____

Two girls with short hair wear glasses and
two girls with long hair wear glasses.

3. How many girls in all wear glasses?

_____ ◯ _____ ☐ _____

Seven of the girls are watching TV.

4. How many of them are sitting up?

_____ ◯ _____ ☐ _____

What's My Number?

How many different names can you find for
a sum?
Make a list to help you predict.

SUM	DIFFERENT NAMES	NUMBER OF NAMES
1	0 + 1 1 + 0	2
2	0 + 2 1 + 1 2 + 0	3
3	0 + 3 1 + 2 3 + 0 2 + 1	4
4	_____ _____	___
5	_____ _____	___
6	_____ _____	___

PREDICT

How many ways can you name each sum?

the sum of 8   ____ names

the sum of 9   ____ names

the sum of 10   ____ names

Changing Rings

Look at the rings.

How many are there? ____

Predict how many addition sentences with 2 addends you can show with these rings. ____ Now write them.

Next to each addition sentence you write,

draw and color the rings to match.

Look at the rings.

How many are there? ____

Predict how many subtraction sentences you can show with these rings. ____ Now write them.

Next to each subtraction sentence you write,

draw and color the rings to match.

Name _____

You need: 2 clothes hangers and 16 clothespins or paper clips.

Take turns.
Think of a subtraction fact.
Show it with clothespins.
Say it out loud.
Write the subtraction fact.
Then show, say, and
write the related fact.

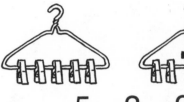

$5 - 2 = 3$

$5 - 3 = 2$

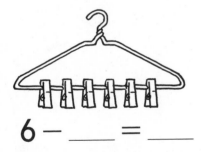

$6 - \underline{\quad} = \underline{\quad}$

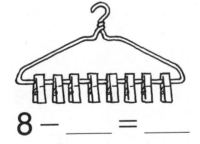

$8 - \underline{\quad} = \underline{\quad}$

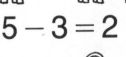

$5 - \underline{\quad} = \underline{\quad}$

Show and write the related facts here.

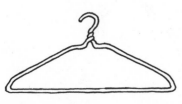

$6 - \underline{\quad} = \underline{\quad}$

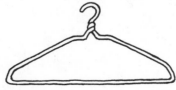

$8 - \underline{\quad} = \underline{\quad}$

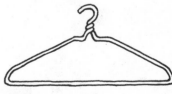

$5 - \underline{\quad} = \underline{\quad}$

Name _____

Flying Kites

Look at the tail on kite 1.
How many bows are shaded? ____ How many are
white? ____ Write the fact family that matches the bows
on the kite. Do the same for kites 2 and 3.
For kite 4, decide how many bows to draw.
Shade some. Leave some white.
Give your page to a friend to write the fact family.

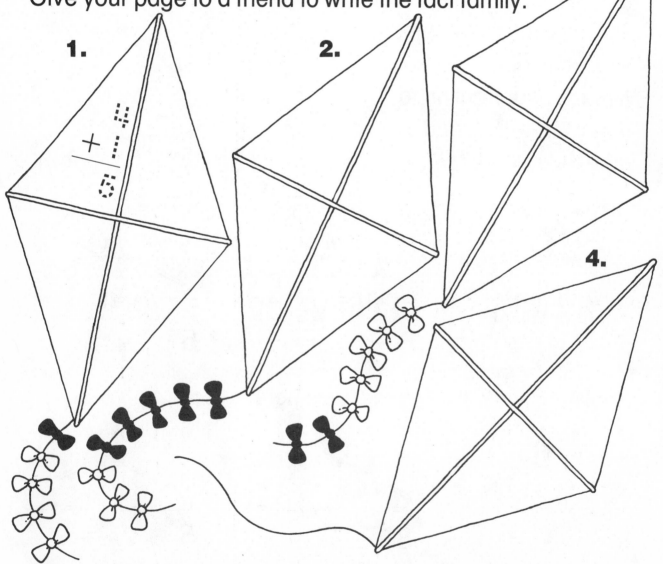

What Is Wrong with This Picture?

Look at each picture.
Ring the things that are wrong. Count them.
Write an addition or subtraction sentence to show
what should be in each picture.

1.

2.

3.

4.

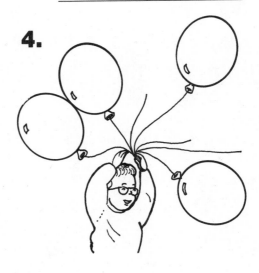

Add in Your Head

Ring the expression that has the greater sum.

1. 6 + 1   or   6 + 2 ?   **2.** 5 + 0   or   5 + 2 ?

3. 2 + 7   or   7 + 3 ?   **4.** 9 + 1   or   0 + 9 ?

Ring the expressions that have the same sum.

5. 2 + 5   6 + 0   4 + 1   4 + 3

6. 9 + 0   7 + 3   2 + 8   0 + 8

7. 3 + 6   9 + 1   7 + 2   7 + 1

8. 5 + 3   5 + 2   8 + 1   0 + 9

Write 0, 1, 2, or 3 in the blank to make
the sentence true.

9. 6 + 2 = 7 + _____

10. 3 + 8 = _____ + 9

11. 4 + 3 = _____ + 7

12. 2 + 7 = 6 + _____

Name _____

Doubles Riddles

Choose a number 1 through 9.

1. My double is 6. Who am I? 3	**2.** My double has two digits. It ends in 0. Who am I? _____
3. My double is between 6 and 10. Who am I? _____	**4.** Double me and you get two digits. One of them is 8. Who am I? _____
5. My double is 14. Who am I? _____	**6.** My double is between 10 and 14. Who am I? _____
7. When you double me, you get 8. Who am I? _____	**8.** Double me and you get 16. Who am I? _____

Name _____

Doubles-Plus-One Coin Count

Ring the coins to show the doubles.
Then write a doubles-plus-one number sentence.
How much money is in each box? ____, ____, ____, ____

1.

_____ + _____ = _____

2.

_____ + _____ = _____

3.

_____ + _____ = _____

4.

_____ + _____ = _____

To the Top

This building has 17 floors.
Pretend that you live on the 5th floor.

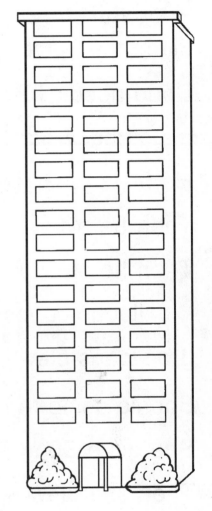

1. You start on your floor.
You go up 5 floors. What
floor are you on?   _____

2. Go up 5 more floors.
What floor are you on?   _____

3. You visit a friend on the
11th floor. How many floors
do you go up from your
floor?   _____

4. You are on floor 7. How
many floors to the top?   _____

Fill in the table.

You are on floor	2	3	9	10	13	11	16
How many to the top?	15						

Blowing Away

Read the story.
Fill in the number sentences as you read.

Doug needs 10 balloons for

his birthday party.

He blew up 3 red balloons.

Then he blew up 4 more.   3 $\bigcirc$ 4 = $\bigcirc$

Then he blew up 3 yellow balloons.   7 $\bigcirc$ 3 = $\bigcirc$

4 balloons popped.   10 $\bigcirc$ 4 = $\bigcirc$

3 balloons blew away.   6 $\bigcirc$ 3 = $\bigcirc$

Bonnie came to help.

She gave Doug 5 green balloons.   3 $\bigcirc$ 5 = $\bigcirc$

Then she blew up 3 more green   8 $\bigcirc$ 3 = $\bigcirc$

balloons, but 3 balloons blew away.   11 $\bigcirc$ 3 = $\bigcirc$

Bonnie blew up 4 more balloons,   8 $\bigcirc$ 4 = $\bigcirc$

but 5 balloons popped.   12 $\bigcirc$ 5 = $\bigcirc$

Doug had a rest.

Then he blew up 4 more balloons.   7 $\bigcirc$ 4 = $\bigcirc$

Does he have enough balloons?   _____

Buying Toys

SALE PRICES

Train	1¢
Car	9¢
Boat	5¢
Plane	4¢
Bike	3¢

Use the sign at the store.
Write what each person bought.

1. Ellen bought 2 toys.
She spent 10¢.
She bought a _____
and a _____ .

2. Peter bought 2 toys.
He spent 8¢.
He bought a _____
and a _____ .

3. Chris spent 7¢.
He bought 2 toys.
He bought a _____
and a _____ .

4. Carmen spent 6¢.
She bought 2 toys.
She bought a _____
and a _____ .

5. You have 10¢.
What can you buy? _____
Will you have change? _____ How much? _____

What Number Am I?

Read each clue.
Write the number.

1. I am between 12 and 15.
I am not equal to 9 + 5.
What number am I? _____

2. I am between 8 and 12.
I am less than 5 + 6.
When you double me you get 18.
What number am I? _____

3. I am more than 9 + 3.
I am less than 9 + 7.
I am not an odd number.
What number am I? _____

4. I am between 10 and 17.
When you add my two digits
you get 6.
What number am I? _____

5. Make up your own clues.
First pick a number. Then write the clues.
Ask a friend to guess your number.

Name _____

Mystery Addends

Make the sums.
Use each number 2 times.
Make number cards and move them around to help.

1.

___	___	___	___
+___	+___	+___	+___
6	5	4	5

2.

___	___	___	___	___
+___	+___	+___	+___	+___
1 2	1 3	1 4	1 4	1 5

Climb the Pyramid

Each number is the sum of
the two numbers below it.
Write the missing numbers.

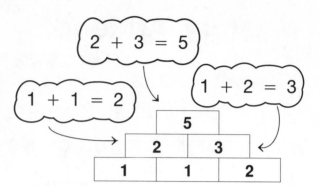

1.

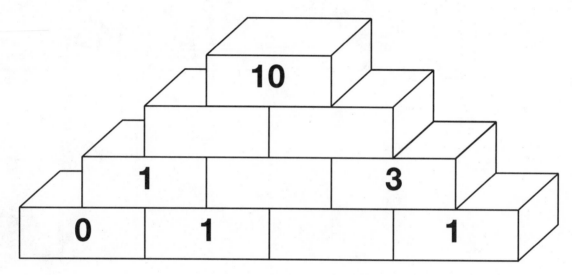

2.

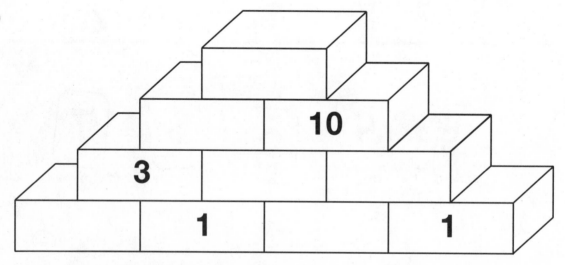

3. On another piece of paper,
make your own pyramid.
Share it with a friend.

Path to a Prize

Choose the correct path.
Draw it.

1.
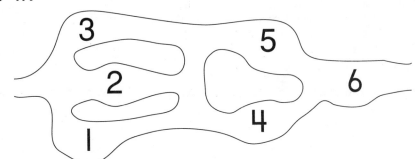

2.
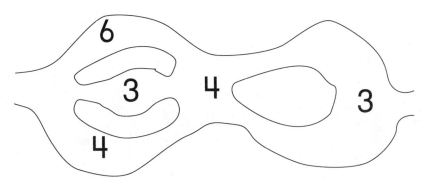

3.
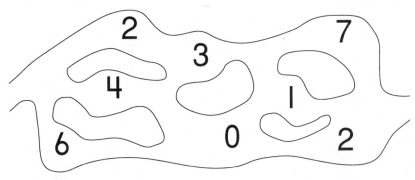

4.
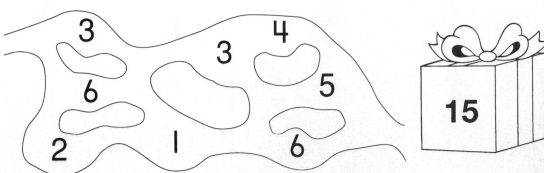

Animals at the Zoo

Dear Family,
    Your child has learned how to ask a question for addition and subtraction stories. Use the picture to tell story problems. Begin a story, such as, "There are 4 monkeys in the trees. There are 3 monkeys on the ground." Have your child ask a question, such as, "How many monkeys are there in all?" Then have your child write the number sentence and solve.

1. _____ ◯ _____ □ _____

2. _____ ◯ _____ □ _____

3. _____ ◯ _____ □ _____

4. _____ ◯ _____ □ _____

Name _____

Patterns to See

Add.

$$\begin{array}{r} 1 \\ +1 \\ \hline \end{array} \qquad \begin{array}{r} 2 \\ +2 \\ \hline \end{array} \qquad \begin{array}{r} 3 \\ +3 \\ \hline \end{array} \qquad \begin{array}{r} 4 \\ +4 \\ \hline \end{array} \qquad \begin{array}{r} 5 \\ +5 \\ \hline \end{array} \qquad \begin{array}{r} 6 \\ +6 \\ \hline \end{array}$$

What is the pattern of the addends? _____

What is the pattern of the sums? _____

Are the sums odd or even? _____

What happens when you add two even numbers? _____

What happens when you add two odd numbers? _____

Add these. Talk about the patterns in the addends and the sums.

$$\begin{array}{r} 4 \\ +5 \\ \hline \end{array} \qquad \begin{array}{r} 5 \\ +6 \\ \hline \end{array} \qquad \begin{array}{r} 6 \\ +7 \\ \hline \end{array} \qquad \begin{array}{r} 7 \\ +8 \\ \hline \end{array} \qquad \begin{array}{r} 8 \\ +9 \\ \hline \end{array} \qquad \begin{array}{r} 9 \\ +10 \\ \hline \end{array}$$

What happens when you add one even number and one

odd number? _____

Try some on your own. See what happens.

Finding Patterns

Read each question.
Find the pattern.
Write the number.

1.

How many windows will this house have?

2.

How many petals?

3.

How many stars?

4.

How many toothpicks?

Colorful Ways

Color the boxes.
Can you finish the pattern?
Use the same colors.

| R = Red |
| O = Orange |
| P = Purple |

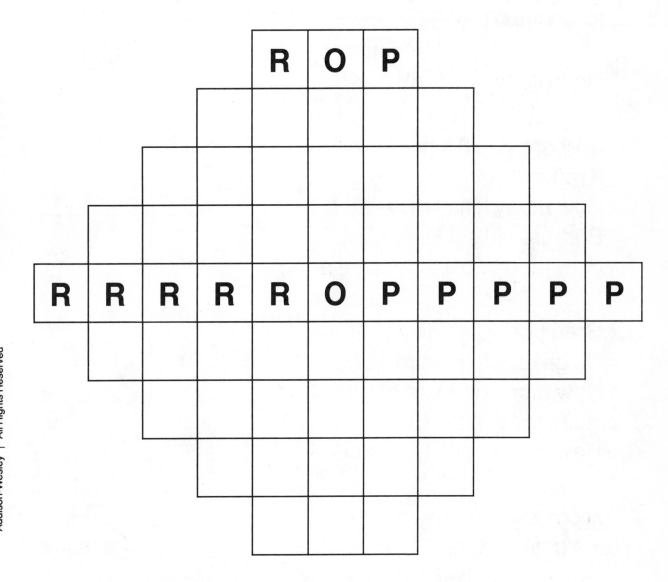

Use colored tiles.
Build your own color pattern.

Pet Problems

Write two number sentences to solve the problem.

1. 2 girls are playing with pets.
2 friends join them.
How many friends in all? _____
They meet 2 more friends.
How many are there now? _____

2. Barbara had 8 kittens.
2 ran away.
How many kittens are left? _____
Barbara sells 3 kittens.
How many does she have now? _____

3. Greg has 10 goldfish.
He gives 4 to his brother.
How many does he have now? _____
He gives 2 to his friend.
How many does Greg keep? _____

4. Rico has 4 gerbils.
He gets 5 more.
How many does he have now? _____
2 gerbils escape.
How many are left? _____

Name _____

Sports Special

Pretend that you work in a sports store.
You keep track of all the things you sell on one Saturday.

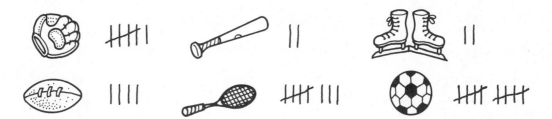

Color the graph to show the data.
Write a title for the graph.

_____
- -
_____

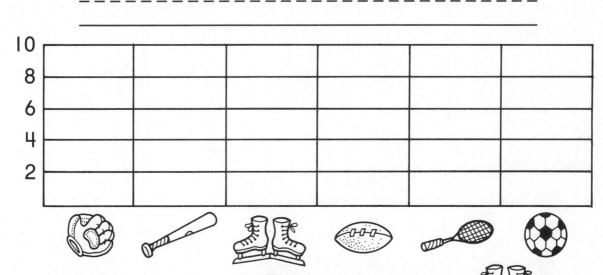

1. How many more  did you sell than 🔺? ____

2. How many fewer 🏏 did you sell than 🥎? ____

3. How many things for baseball did you sell? ____

4. How many balls in all did you sell? ____

Name _____

Taking a Survey

Matt took a survey.

He asked 25 people which fruit they like best.

Matt made a graph to show the data.

FAVORITE FRUIT

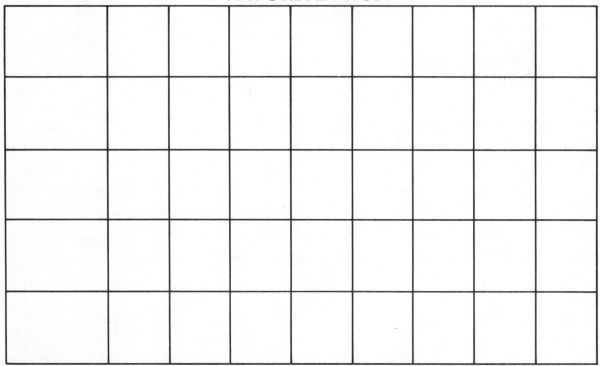

Help Matt finish the graph.

He found out that the favorite fruit was .

The least favorite fruit was  .

The same number of people picked and .

Cut out the pictures.

Paste them on the graph to match the data.

   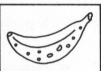 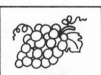

The Robot Factory

These graphs show how many robots the robot teams made at the robot factory. Use the graphs to answer the questions. Each 🤖 stands for 2 robots.

Month 1

Blue Team	🤖 🤖 🤖
Red Team	🤖 🤖
Green Team	🤖

Month 2

Blue Team	🤖 🤖
Red Team	🤖 🤖 🤖 🤖 🤖
Green Team	🤖 🤖

1. Which team made the most robots in Month 1?

_____

2. In which month did the Green Team make more robots? _____ How many more? _____

3. Which team made the most robots in all? _____

4. How many robots were made in Month 2? _____

Make a graph for Month 3.
Use the data in the box.

Month 3

Blue Team	
Red Team	
Green Team	

The Green Team made 4 more robots than they made in Month 1.

The Red Team made 4 fewer robots than they did in Month 2.

The Blue Team made the same number of robots as they made in Month 1.

Missing Numbers

Fill in the missing data to tell the story.
Then tell the story a different way.

1. Ann has 7 baseball caps, some blue and some red.

_____ are blue and

_____ are red.

Ann has 7 baseball caps, some blue and some red.

_____ are blue and

_____ are red.

---

2. One team beat the other team by 4 points.

The score was ___ to ___.

One team beat the other team by 4 points.

The score was ___ to ___.

---

3. Carol is in charge of 8 mitts.

_____ are left-hand mitts.

_____ are right-hand mitts.

Carol is in charge of 8 mitts.

_____ are left-hand mitts.

_____ are right-hand mitts.

---

4. Drew had cold drinks for the 18 players.

_____ wanted orange juice.

_____ wanted grape juice.

Drew had cold drinks for the 18 players.

_____ wanted orange juice.

_____ wanted grape juice.

Name _____

Calculator Subtraction

Use your 🖩 . Press the keys in order.
Write the numbers you see.

1. Count back by 1s from 7.

ON/C	7	−	1	=	=	=	=	=	=	=

___ ___ ___ ___ ___ ___ ___

How many times did you press [=]? _7_

Write the subtraction sentence. _7_ − _7_ = _0_

2. Count back by 1s from 10.

ON/C	10	−	1	=	=	=

___ ___ ___

How many times did you press [=]? ___

Write the subtraction sentence. ___ − ___ = ___

3. Count back by 1s from 5.

ON/C	5	−	1	=	=	=	=	=

___ ___ ___ ___ ___

How many times did you press [=]? ___

Write the subtraction sentence. ___ − ___ = ___

Name _____

Double Two = Four

Read each question.
Write the subtraction sentence.
Write the add-to-check fact.

What is double two less double one?

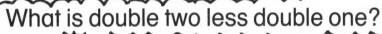

$$4 - 2 = 2 \qquad 2 + 2 = 4$$

---

1. What is double four less double two?

---

2. What is double six less double three?

---

3. What is double five less double two plus one?

---

4. What is double nine less double four plus one?

---

5. Make up your own. Give it to a friend to solve.

Make a Number Pattern

Subtract.

$10 - 3 =$ ___ $10 - 5 =$ ___ $10 - 6 =$ ___

$10 - 8 =$ ___ $10 - 7 =$ ___ $10 - 4 =$ ___

1. Write the exercises above in order from the smallest difference to the largest difference.

___   ___   ___   ___   ___   ___
___   ___   ___   ___   ___   ___
___   ___   ___   ___   ___   ___

2. What pattern do you see? Check one.

Each time you take away one less, the difference is one less. ☐

Each time you take away one less, the difference is one more. ☐

3. Subtract from 9. Make the same pattern as the one in Exercise 1.

$$\begin{array}{r} 9 \\ -7 \\ \hline 2 \end{array}$$

4. Look at the two sets of exercises.
Talk about the patterns with a partner.

Name _____

Sea Story

Look at the picture.
Write a number sentence
to answer each question.

The divers see a school of 🐟 .

1. How many more angelfish are there than divers?

_____ ⊖ _____ ☐= _____

The 🐢 and the 🦀 have shells.

2. How many more hermit crabs are there than turtles?

_____ ⊖ _____ ☐= _____

One diver has a 📷

3. How many divers do not have cameras?

_____ ⊖ _____ ☐= _____

4. How many more 🐟 are there than 🦀 ?

_____ ⊖ _____ ☐= _____

Which One?

1. Ring facts with a difference of 1.
Tell how you know. Subtract to check.

$$\begin{array}{r} 7 \\ -6 \\ \hline \end{array} \qquad \begin{array}{r} 8 \\ -6 \\ \hline \end{array} \qquad \begin{array}{r} 4 \\ -1 \\ \hline \end{array} \qquad \begin{array}{r} 5 \\ -4 \\ \hline \end{array} \qquad \begin{array}{r} 9 \\ -8 \\ \hline \end{array}$$

$$\begin{array}{r} 8 \\ -5 \\ \hline \end{array} \qquad \begin{array}{r} 11 \\ -10 \\ \hline \end{array} \qquad \begin{array}{r} 8 \\ -7 \\ \hline \end{array} \qquad \begin{array}{r} 10 \\ -8 \\ \hline \end{array} \qquad \begin{array}{r} 11 \\ -9 \\ \hline \end{array}$$

Ring the larger difference. Tell how you know.

2.
$$\begin{array}{r} 9 \\ -6 \\ \hline \end{array}$$ or $$\begin{array}{r} 9 \\ -1 \\ \hline \end{array}$$

3.
$$\begin{array}{r} 7 \\ -5 \\ \hline \end{array}$$ or $$\begin{array}{r} 7 \\ -6 \\ \hline \end{array}$$

4.
$$\begin{array}{r} 11 \\ -8 \\ \hline \end{array}$$ or $$\begin{array}{r} 11 \\ -10 \\ \hline \end{array}$$

5.
$$\begin{array}{r} 12 \\ -9 \\ \hline \end{array}$$ or $$\begin{array}{r} 10 \\ -3 \\ \hline \end{array}$$

Name _____

Subtraction Riddles

Can you find the mystery numbers?

1. When you subtract me from 12, you get 9. Who am I?

2. When you subtract 8 from me, you get 4. Who am I?

_____

3. When you subtract 3 from me, you get 9. Who am I?

_____

4. When you subtract me from 11, you get 5. Who am I?

_____

5. You get me when you subtract a number from itself. Who am I?

_____

6. When you subtract 5 from me and add 1, you get 6. Who am I?

_____

Now make a mystery number riddle of your own!

_____   Who am I?

_____   _____

_____   _____

Name _____

Relate the Facts

1. Write four subtraction sentences.
Use these numbers only.

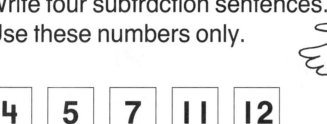

$$11 - 4 = 7$$

___ − ___ = ___

___ − ___ = ___   ___ − ___ = ___

2. Write five subtraction
sentences.
Use these numbers only.

___ − ___ = ___   ___ − ___ = ___

___ − ___ = ___   ___ − ___ = ___

___ − ___ = ___

3. Write six subtraction
sentences.
Use these numbers only.

___ − ___ = ___   ___ − ___ = ___

___ − ___ = ___   ___ − ___ = ___

___ − ___ = ___   ___ − ___ = ___

Name _____

Fact Families

Read each story.
Think it through.
Write your answers on the lines.
Write the children's ages on the T-shirts below.

1. Ben is 2. Bob is 9
years older than Ben.
Bill is 2 years younger
than Bob.

Think it through.
Ben   _____ years old
Bob   _____ + 2 = _____
Bill   _____ − 2 = _____

---

2. Jane is 7. Her sister
Jill is 5 years older.
Joy is 7 years
younger than Jill.

Think it through.
Jane   _____ years old
Jill   _____ + 7 = _____
Joy   _____ − 7 = _____

---

3. Bill's cat is 3 years
old. Jane's rabbit is
3 years older than
Bill's cat. Jill's dog
is 3 years younger
than Jane's rabbit.

Think it through.
cat   _____ years old
rabbit   _____ + 3 = _____
dog   _____ − 3 = _____

BEN   BOB   BILL   JANE   JILL   JOY

Name _____

Work Wheel

Use the work wheel
to answer the questions.

1. Which two jobs would earn the most? _____

_____

2. Which two jobs would earn the least? _____

_____

3. Jane earned 15¢ last week. Which two jobs did she do?

_____

4. Sam earned 6¢ less than Jane. Which job did he do?

_____

5. Adam did two jobs. He earned 16¢. One job was
collecting milk money. What was the other?

_____

6. Which two jobs would earn less than 18¢ and more
than 16¢?

_____

What Is Next?

Subtract.

9	9	11	11	13	13
−9	−8	−9	−8	−9	−8

What patterns do you see?

_____

_____

Subtract. Write the next two number facts in the pattern.

14	14	14	11	__	__
−7	−8	−9	−7	−__	−__

What patterns do you see?

_____

_____

Fill in numbers to make up your own pattern.

__	__	__	__	__	__
−9	−9	−9	−9	−9	−9
__	__	__	__	__	__

Name _____

How Much More?

Look at the coins in each hand.
How much more money do you need to buy each toy?
Choose the coins you need from the ones pictured below.

Toy	I Have	I Need

1.

12¢ _____ _____

2.

13¢ _____ _____

3.

15¢ _____ _____

Name _____

Party Facts

Read the stories. Write the missing number on the line.
Complete the number sentences at the right of each story.
Match the story with its number sentence.

1.

Jeff wrote sixteen party
invitations. He mailed eight of
them. Jeff has ____ left to mail.

$16 - 8 = \underline{\ 8\ }$

$16 - 0 = \underline{\ 16\ }$

$8 - 8 = \underline{\ 0\ }$

2.

Cassie drew twelve witches.
She cut out five of them.

Cassie has ____ left to cut out.

$12 - 7 = \underline{\ 5\ }$

$12 - 5 = \underline{\ 7\ }$

$7 - 5 = \underline{\ 2\ }$

3.

Nancy has eleven pumpkins.
She carved seven of them.

Nancy has ____ more
pumpkins to carve.

$11 - 7 = \underline{\ 4\ }$

$11 - 4 = \underline{\ 7\ }$

$7 - 4 = \underline{\ 3\ }$

4.

Steve put fourteen apples in
the tub. His friends bobbed for
nine of them. Now ____ apples
are left.

$14 - 5 = \underline{\ 9\ }$

$9 - 5 = \underline{\ 4\ }$

$14 - 9 = \underline{\ 5\ }$

5. What kind of party is it? _____

Name _____

Mental Math

Dear Family,
   Your child is learning to use mental math to solve problems. Help your child use the clues below to find the pearls.

1. A big pearl is in the oyster that is the sum of a double. It is more than 8 + 9.

   The sum of its digits is _____.

   The big pearl is in oyster _____.

2. A middle-sized pearl is in the oyster that is less than 15 − 2. It is a 1-digit number.

   It is more than double 4 and less than double _____.

   The middle-sized pearl is in oyster _____.

3. A small pearl is in the oyster that is more than 7 + 3. The sum of the digits is less than 14 − 5.

   One digit is _____.

   The small pearl is in oyster _____.

Mystery Numbers

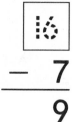

$$16 - 7 = 9$$

$$\begin{array}{r} 16 \\ -\ 7 \\ \hline 9 \end{array}$$

Write the missing numbers.

1.
$$\begin{array}{r} \boxed{13} \\ -\ 9 \\ \hline 4 \end{array} \qquad \begin{array}{r} \square \\ -\ 7 \\ \hline 9 \end{array} \qquad \begin{array}{r} \square \\ -\ 6 \\ \hline 6 \end{array} \qquad \begin{array}{r} \square \\ -\ 9 \\ \hline 6 \end{array} \qquad \begin{array}{r} \square \\ -\ 7 \\ \hline 6 \end{array}$$

2.
$$\begin{array}{r} \square \\ -\ 5 \\ \hline 8 \end{array} \qquad \begin{array}{r} \square \\ -\ 8 \\ \hline 7 \end{array} \qquad \begin{array}{r} \square \\ -\ 8 \\ \hline 4 \end{array} \qquad \begin{array}{r} \square \\ -\ 9 \\ \hline 9 \end{array} \qquad \begin{array}{r} \square \\ -\ 8 \\ \hline 3 \end{array}$$

3.
$$\begin{array}{r} \square \\ -\ 4 \\ \hline 7 \end{array} \qquad \begin{array}{r} \square \\ -\ 8 \\ \hline 9 \end{array} \qquad \begin{array}{r} \square \\ -\ 8 \\ \hline 5 \end{array} \qquad \begin{array}{r} \square \\ -\ 6 \\ \hline 8 \end{array} \qquad \begin{array}{r} \square \\ -\ 6 \\ \hline 9 \end{array}$$

4.
$$\begin{array}{r} \square \\ -\ 7 \\ \hline 8 \end{array} \qquad \begin{array}{r} \square \\ -\ 6 \\ \hline 7 \end{array} \qquad \begin{array}{r} \square \\ -\ 9 \\ \hline 7 \end{array} \qquad \begin{array}{r} \square \\ -\ 7 \\ \hline 5 \end{array} \qquad \begin{array}{r} \square \\ -\ 9 \\ \hline 8 \end{array}$$

Name _____

Math Machine

Here is how the Math Machine works:

The card
goes in with
a number.

In 10 -6 Out 4

The card
comes out
with the answer.

This happens.

Some of the math machines below are broken. Find them.
Each broken machine can be fixed by changing one of the
3 numbers. Choose one to change in each machine.

In 13 -4 Out 8

In 15 -9 Out 7

In 14 -8 Out 6

In 12 -5 Out 7

In 11 -6 Out 2

In 16 -7 Out 8

In The Family

Think of the fact family.

Cross out the number that does not belong.

1.

7   6

13   5

2.

5   15

14   9

3.

6   15

9   13

4.

8   13

5   14

5.

6   4

7   11

6.

9   6

10   4

Cross out the two numbers that do not belong.

7.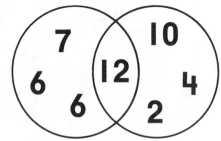

7   10

6   12   4

6   2

8.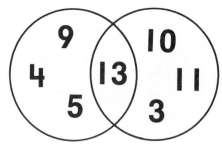

9   10

4   13   11

5   3

9.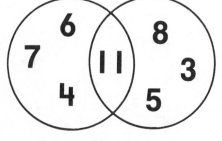

6   8

7   11   3

4   5

10.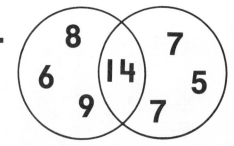

8   7

6   14   5

9   7

Name _____

Grocery Shopping

Read the story. Draw a picture to help solve it. Make an X for each item. Then answer the questions below.

Rob and Rebecca went to the market. They each took a cart. Rob got 3 loaves of bread, 1 jar of peanut butter, 6 bananas, 2 boxes of cereal, 4 packages of cheese, 2 cartons of milk, and 3 bottles of juice. Rebecca put 4 packages of napkins, 3 packs of paper plates, and 2 boxes of spoons in her cart.

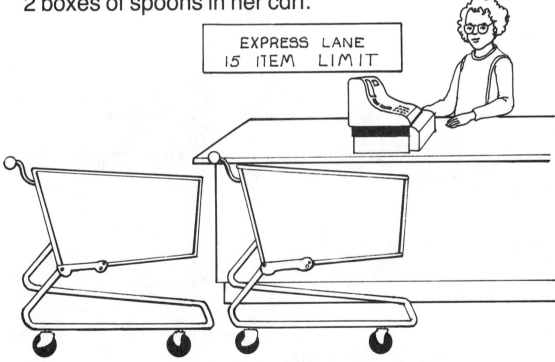

EXPRESS LANE
15 ITEM LIMIT

1. How many items did Rob put in his cart? _____

2. How many items did Rebecca put in her cart? _____

3. How many items should Rob put in Rebecca's cart so they can both use the express lane? _____

Name _____

Ways to Measure

Think about measuring each object.
Ring the better unit of measure to use.

1.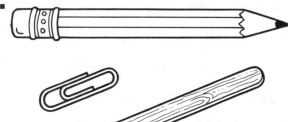

2.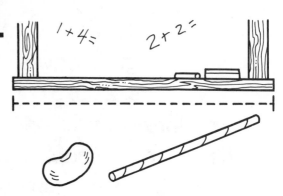

3.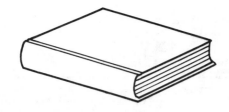

4.

5. Maria measured her desktop.
Ring the measurement that does not make sense.

19 paperclips   32 cubes   15 straws   10 toothpicks

Name _____

Measure, Think, and Write

Use your inch ruler.
Find the length to the nearest $\frac{1}{2}$ inch.

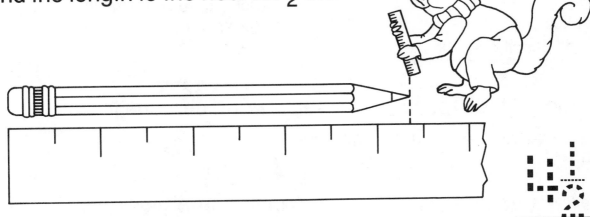

1.

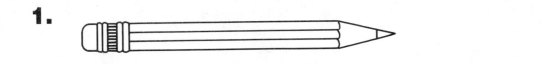

_____

2.

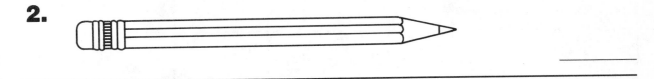

_____

3.

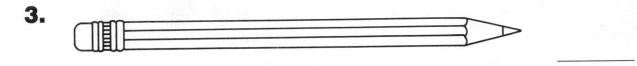

_____

4.

_____

5.

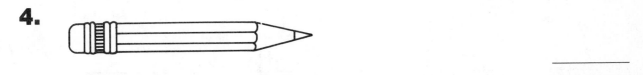

_____

Wearing Out Graph

Ted measured his pencils and crayons.

black pencil = 8 inches	purple crayon = 3 inches
blue pencil = 6 inches	brown crayon = 4 inches
red pencil = 7 inches	

Imagine that Ted uses his pencils and crayons for a while.

Now each pencil is 2 inches shorter.

Each crayon is 1 inch shorter.

Draw each pencil and crayon on the graph

to show the length it is now.

Use the colors on Ted's list.

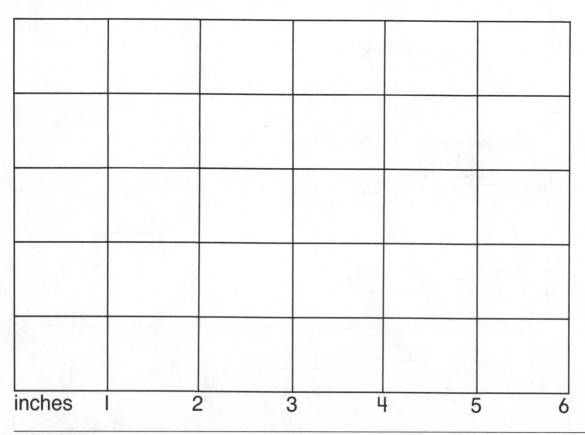

inches   1   2   3   4   5   6

String Curves

You will need a piece of string, a ruler, and a curved object to measure, such as a ball or a vase.

Step 1	Step 2

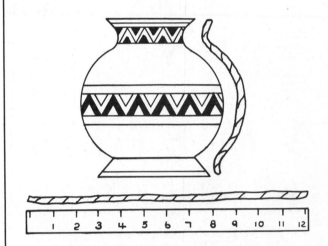

Estimate the length of the curve.

about __10__ inches

Use your string to measure. Then place the string on a ruler to find the length in inches.

__12__ inches

Choose 2 curved objects to measure.

1. Object: _____

　　Estimate: _____ in.

　　Measure: _____ in.

2. Object: _____

　　Estimate: _____ in.

　　Measure: _____ in.

Name _____

Choosing Units

Write **feet** if you would measure in feet.
Write **yards** if you would measure in yards.

1. Your leg _____

2. The length of a soccer field _____

3. How far you can jump _____

4. Your height _____

5. The length of your desk _____

6. A running track _____

Write **foot**, **feet**, or **yards** to complete each sentence.

7. The runner is about 6 _____ tall.

8. The distance from the runner's heel to his

    toe is about 1 _____ .

9. It took the runner 1 minute to run 100 _____ .

10. The length of his arm is about 2 _____ .

11. One lap around the track is 440 _____ .

Are You Sure?

The Peters family is not too sure about measuring.

Tell whether each is possible or not possible.
Write **yes** or **no**.

1. Nina pours 1 quart of juice into 2 pint jars. _____

2. Chris pours 1 quart of milk into a cup. _____

3. Misty the kitten drinks 1 quart

   of water at once. _____

4. Dad washes all of the dishes in

   1 pint of water. _____

5. Aaron drinks 6 quarts of water at lunch. _____

6. Mom made tea in 1 cup. _____

7. In one week the family uses only

   1 quart of water. _____

Weighing Zoo Friends

It is weigh-in time at the Children's Zoo.
The results are on graph.

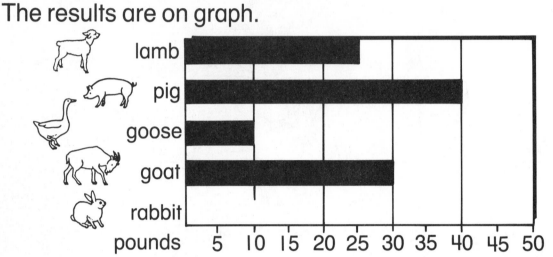

1. The rabbit weighs about 15 pounds. Fill in the graph.

2. Which animal weighs almost as much as the

   goat? _____

3. How much will the pig weigh if it gains 10

   pounds? _____

4. What is the weight of the rabbit and the

   goose together? _____

5. Together the goose and the goat weigh the

   same as the _____ .

6. Together the rabbit and the goose weigh

   the same as the _____ .

A Mouse Walk

The mice must stay on a line.

They can go right or down.

Each one goes 16 centimeters in all.

How many different paths can you find?

Two paths are shown.

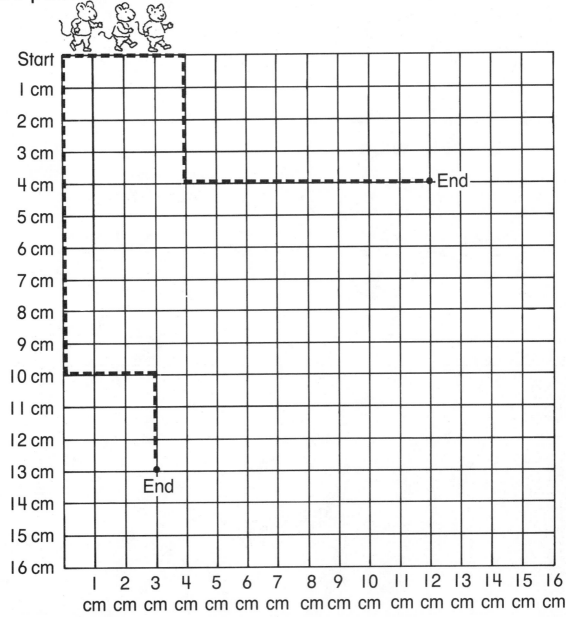

Estimate It

Name three items for each measurement.

1. about 2 decimeters long

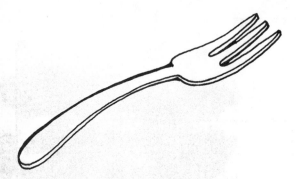

_____

_____

_____

2. about 1 meter wide

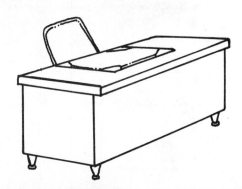

_____

_____

_____

3. about 2 meters tall

_____

_____

_____

Name _____

Balancing Act

1. Ring the item you would need the most of
to balance the scale.

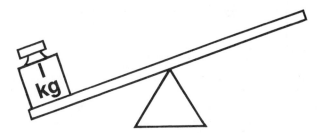   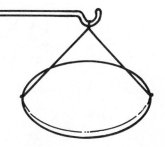

2. Write how many of each you would need
to balance the scale.
Use these numbers.

4	9	1

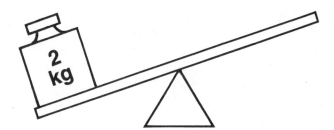  

_____   _____   _____

3. Balance the scale.   2 kg   1 kg   3 kg
Use all the weights once.   8 kg   4 kg
Write the weights on the scale.

At what weight is the scale balanced? _____

Zegs and Zogs

1. These are zegs.   These are <u>not</u> zegs.

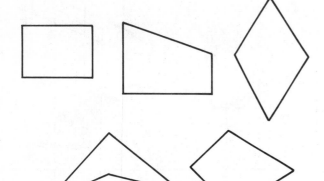
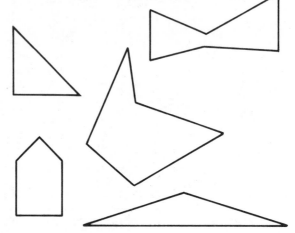

Is this a zeg? Ring yes or no.

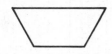

          yes   no

2. These are zogs.   These are <u>not</u> zogs.

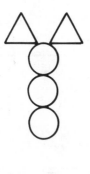

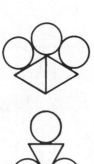

Is this a zog?

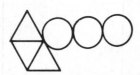

          yes   no

Name _____

Guess and Count

Estimate the number of tens and ones.
Ring tens and count to check.

1. △ △ △ △ △
△ △ △ △ △
△ △ △ △ △
△ △ △ △ △
△ △ △ △

Guess	
Tens	Ones

Count	
Tens	Ones

2. ○ ○ ○ ○ ○
○ ○ ○ ○ ○
○ ○ ○ ○ ○
○ ○ ○ ○ ○
○ ○ ○ ○ ○
○ ○ ○ ○ ○
○ ○ ○ ○
○ ○ ○ ○
○ ○ ○ ○

Guess	
Tens	Ones

Count	
Tens	Ones

3.

Guess	
Tens	Ones

Count	
Tens	Ones

4. ☆ ☆
☆ ☆ ☆ ☆ ☆
☆ ☆ ☆ ☆ ☆
☆ ☆ ☆ ☆ ☆ ☆ ☆ ☆ ☆
☆ ☆ ☆ ☆ ☆ ☆ ☆ ☆ ☆
☆ ☆ ☆ ☆ ☆
☆ ☆ ☆ ☆ ☆
☆ ☆

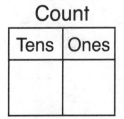

Guess	
Tens	Ones

Count	
Tens	Ones

What Is In the Box?

How many tens and ones are left in the box?

 This many in all.

1.

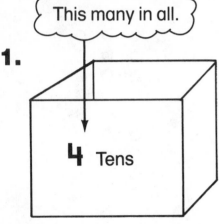

This many are out of the box.

4 Tens

_____
- - - - - - - - - - - - - - - - - - -
_____

2.

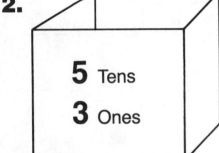

5 Tens
3 Ones

_____
- - - - - - - - - - - - - - - - - - -
_____

3.

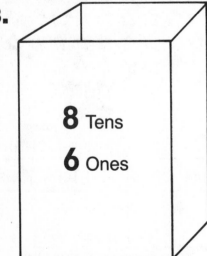

8 Tens
6 Ones

_____
- - - - - - - - - - - - - - - - - - -
_____
- - - - - - - - - - - - - - - - - - -
_____

Name _____

More or Less

Ring the number.

1.	It is more than 50.	thirty	fifty
	It is less than 70.	forty	sixty
2.	It is more than 60.	sixty	eighty
	It is less than 80.	seventy	ninety
3.	It is the smallest number given.	twenty	forty
		thirty	fifty
4.	It is between 20 and 60.	twenty	sixty
		forty	ten
5.	It is more than 40.	thirty	seventy
	It is less than 60.	fifty	ninety

Make a New Number

1. How many 2-digit numbers can you make with these cards?
Do not use doubles (22, 55, 44).

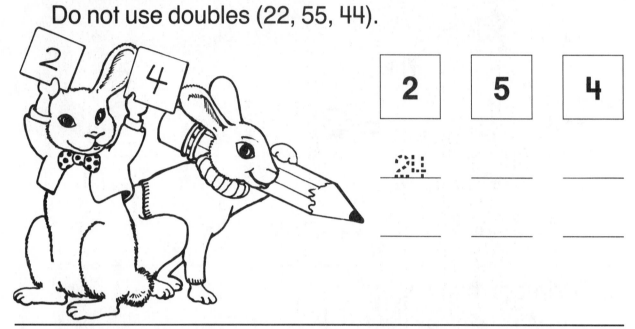

2	**5**	**4**
24	___	___
___	___	___

2. Write all the 2-digit numbers you can make with these cards.
Do not use doubles (11, 33, 66, 88).

1	**3**	**6**	**8**
___	___	___	___
___	___	___	___
___	___	___	___

Name _____

Packing Up

Mike has sorted his books.
Now he has to pack them up.
Which box should he put each group of books in?
Draw lines to match.

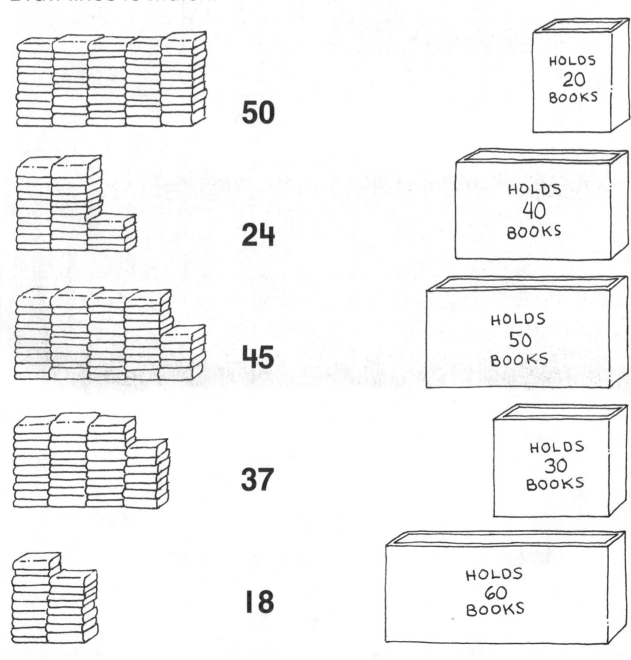

50

24

45

37

18

HOLDS 20 BOOKS

HOLDS 40 BOOKS

HOLDS 50 BOOKS

HOLDS 30 BOOKS

HOLDS 60 BOOKS

Name _____

Thinking Money

How much money is there?

1. 3 more dimes than
pennies

2 pennies

_____ ¢

2. 4 more dimes than
pennies

I penny

_____ ¢

3. 2 fewer pennies than
dimes

5 dimes

_____ ¢

4. Same number of dimes
and pennies

4 dimes

_____ ¢

5. 5 fewer pennies than
dimes

5 dimes

_____ ¢

6. 6 more pennies than
dimes

4 dimes

_____ ¢

7. 8 more pennies than
dimes

2 dimes

_____ ¢

8. 4 fewer pennies than
dimes

5 dimes

_____ ¢

Use with text pages 147 – 148.

Name _____

Riddles

Read the number riddle.
Match the riddle to the number.

1. I have a 3 in the ones place.
I have an 8 in the tens place.
Who am I?

seventy-six

2. I have a 5 in the tens place.
I have a 1 in the ones place.
Who am I?

fifty-one

3. My ones place is one more than
5. My tens place is one less
than 8. Who am I?

seventy-seven

4. My tens place is one more than
3. My ones place is one more
than 6. Who am I?

forty-seven

5. I have two more than 5 in my
ones place. I have 3 more than
4 in my tens place. Who am I?

fifty-two

6. I have two more than 3 in my tens
place. I have two less than 4 in
my ones place. Who am I?

eighty-three

Name _____

Beans, Beans, Beans

How many beans are there?

Here is an easy way to find out.

▶ Put a ring around 10 beans. ▶ Put a box around 10 rings.

1. How many hundreds (boxes)? _____

2. How many extra tens (rings)? _____

3. How many extra ones (beans)? _____

4. How many beans in all? _____

Name _____

Lemonade Sales

Peter sold lemonade for 10¢ a glass.
On Monday he sold 4 glasses. On Tuesday he sold 2 fewer glasses. On Wednesday he sold 5 glasses. On Thursday he sold the same number of glasses as he did on Monday.
On Friday Peter sold 2 more glasses than on Wednesday.
Color the graph to match the data.

Color 1 for each 10¢ Peter earned.

Monday	🪙 🪙 🪙 🪙 🪙 🪙 🪙
Tuesday	🪙 🪙 🪙 🪙 🪙 🪙 🪙
Wednesday	🪙 🪙 🪙 🪙 🪙 🪙 🪙
Thursday	🪙 🪙 🪙 🪙 🪙 🪙 🪙
Friday	🪙 🪙 🪙 🪙 🪙 🪙 🪙

Ring the answer.

1. On which day did Peter earn the most money?

Wednesday   Friday   Monday

2. On which day did he earn the least?

Monday   Tuesday   Thursday

3. How much did Peter earn in the first 2 days?

40¢   60¢   90¢

Pathmaker

Play with a partner. Each needs a game sheet.
You also need 2 number cubes: 1 – 6 and 4 – 9.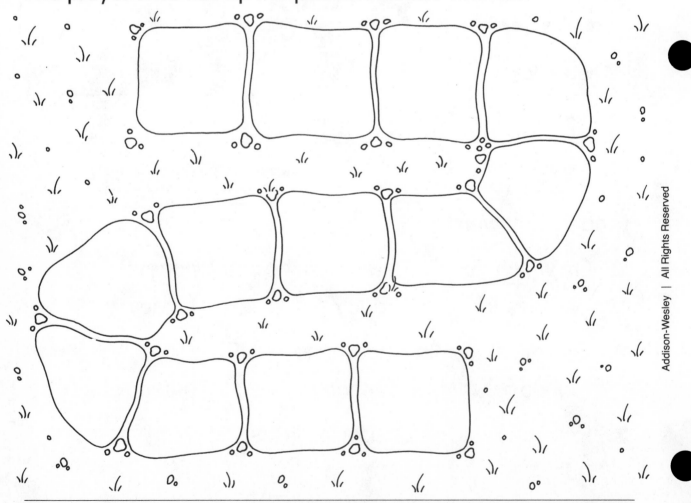
Take turns. Roll both cubes.
Choose your number. If you roll , choose 64 or 46.
Write the number on one of the stones.
Every time you roll a number, write it in order
(before or after) on the path. If there is no empty stone
before or after, you lose your turn.
The player who fills up the path first is the winner.

Puzzle Pages

Amy, Bob, Cal, and Dina have the same puzzle book.

1. Amy is on page 44.
Bob is on the next page.

What page is Bob on? ____

Did you count on or count back? _____

2. Dina is doing a puzzle on page 32.
Cal is on the page before.

What page is Cal on? ____

Did you count on or count back? _____

3. Amy colored the picture on page 57.
Dina gave her the crayons she had used
on the page before.

On which page did Dina use crayons? ____

Did you count on or count back? _____

4. Bob wants to cut out page 83 to make an airplane.
So he did the next page first.

What page did Bob do first? ____

Did you count on or count back? _____

Reading a Bus Schedule

The buses leave every 10 minutes.
Count on or count back by 10s to finish the chart.

After School Bus Schedule		
Red Bus To: Scouts	Blue Bus To: Art Class	Orange Bus To: Dance Center
3:05	3:____	3:____
3:_15_	3:28	3:____
3:____	3:____	3:____
3:____	3:____	3:51

Use the schedule to answer the questions.

1. What time is the first bus to the art class? 3:____

2. What time is the first bus to the Dance Center? 3:____

3. What time is the last bus to Scouts? 3:____

4. Wendy goes to dance class after school.
   Her school day ends at 3:25.
   What time is the first bus she can take? 3:____

5. Eddie goes to Scouts today.
   He leaves school at 3:20.
   Which bus will get him to Scouts the soonest? 3:____

Least Number, Greatest Number

Write the least number.
Write the greatest number.

1. Use these number cards.

least   greatest

2. Use these number cards.

least   greatest

3. Use these number cards.

least   greatest

4. Use these number cards.

least   greatest

Name _____

Fruity Problems

Use the data on the sign.
Add or subtract in your head. Write the answer.

 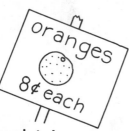  

apples 13¢ each   oranges 8¢ each   cherries 4¢ each   plums 7¢ each   bananas 11¢ each

1. Ann bought 1 orange and 1 cherry. How much did she spend?

_____

2. Ray had 10¢. He bought a plum. How much does he have left?

_____

3. Tara gave 15¢ for an apple. How much change should she get?

_____

4. Hank bought 2 oranges. How much did he spend?

_____

5. How much more for a banana than an orange?

_____

6. How much more for an apple than a plum?

_____

7. How much for 3 cherries?

_____

8. How much more for 2 oranges than 1 apple?

_____

Mystery Numbers

Can you find the mystery numbers?

1. I am between 4 and 8.
You say me when you
skip count by 2s.

Who am I?

___

2. I am more than 15.
I am less than 21.
You say me when you
skip count by 3s.
Who am I?

___

3. I am less than 40.
I am more than 32.
You say me when you
skip count by 4s.
Who am I?

___

4. I am between 28
and 32.
You say me when you
skip count by 2s.
Who am I?

___

5. I am less than 48.
I am more than 40.
You say me when you
skip count by 4s.
Who am I?

___

6. I am between 24
and 30.
You say me when you
skip count by 3s.
Who am I?

___

Now make a mystery number riddle of your own!

_____ Who am I?

Name _____

Fast Fives

Use your .

Press the keys in order. Write the numbers you see.

1. Count forward by 5s.

| ON/C | 5 | + | 5 | = | = | = | = | = | = |

---

2. Count forward by 5s.

| ON/C | 25 | + | 5 | = | = | = | = | = | = |

---

3. Count forward by 5s.

| ON/C | 50 | + | 5 | = | = | = | = | = | = |

---

4. Count forward by 5s.

| ON/C | 75 | + | 5 | = | = | = | = | = | = |

---

5. Count forward by 25s.

| ON/C | 25 | + | 25 | = | = | = | = | = | = |

Who's on First?

Read the clues to find the batting order.
1st is on the card of the player who is up first.
Write 2nd, 3rd, 4th, 5th, 6th, 7th, 8th, 9th, 10th, and
11th on the other cards.

Clues: The first player on the bench bats third.
The second player bats seventh.
The fourth girl bats eighth.
The second girl bats fifth.
The last player on the bench bats fourth.
The fifth boy bats second.
The second boy bats ninth.
The sixth player bats eleventh.
The third girl bats tenth.
The next to last player bats sixth.

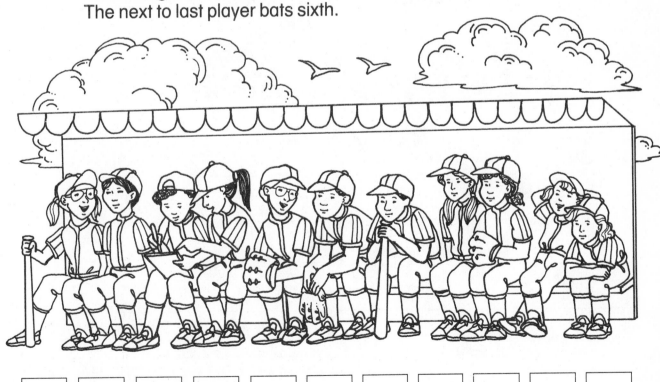

   1st

A New Story

Read the story. Write a number sentence and complete the answer. Draw a line under the extra data.

John has 9 toy cars. Gary has 6 toy cars.
3 of Gary's cars are blue.
How many of Gary's cars are not blue?

_____   _____ cars are not blue.

Reread the story. Think of another question you could ask.
Write the story and the question.
Leave out the data that is extra this time.
Write a number sentence and the answer.

_____

_____

_____

_____

_____

_____

Name _____

No Time to Loaf

Jo, Jan, and Jim are baking bread. They began at 3:05. Look at the clock in each picture. How many minutes did each step take?

1. Jan mixed the ingredients.
From: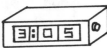

To: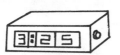

It took ____ minutes.

2. They let the dough rest.
From: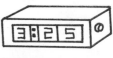

To:

It rested ____ minutes.

3. Jim kneaded the dough.
From:

To: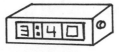

He kneaded ____ minutes.

4. Jo kneaded it, too.
From:

To: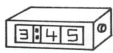

She kneaded ____ minutes.

5. They let the dough rise.
From:

To:

That took ____ hours.

6. They put it in the oven.
From: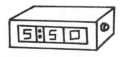

To:

It baked ____ minutes.

Name _____

Time for Field Day

Write the time for each event.
Draw a path from the gate to each event beginning
with the earliest time. Continue until you reach
the latest time.

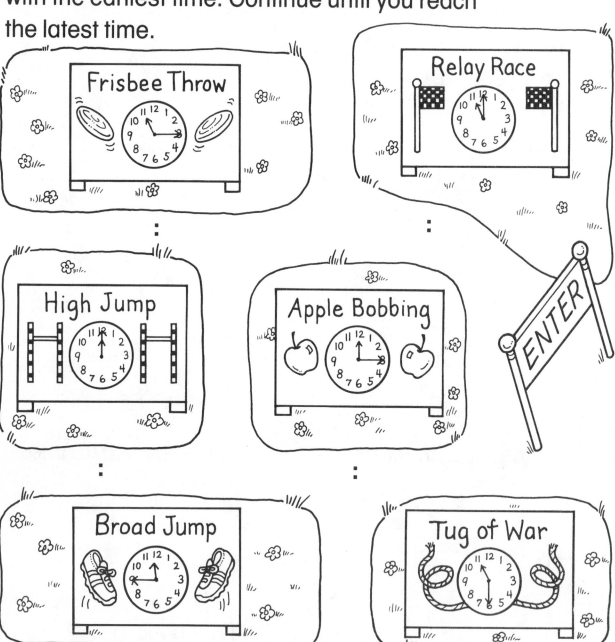

Name _____

Circus Time

Look at the clock next to each ride.
Read the sign.
Decide when the ride will open.
Write the time.
Which ride will open first?
Number the rides in order from 1 to 5.

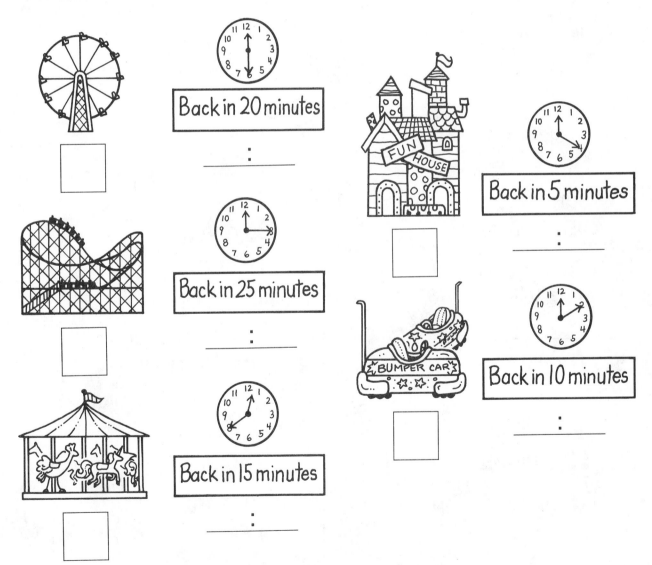

The Time Was . . .

Read each story.
Then draw hands on each clock.

1. The time was →

Patty read for
30 minutes.

Then the
time was ⟶

2. The time was →

Bill swam for
an hour.

Then the
time was ⟶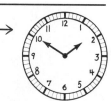

3. The time was →

Jane played for
45 minutes.

Then the
time was ⟶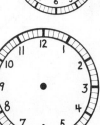

4. The time was →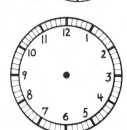

Tim slept for
30 minutes.

Then the
time was ⟶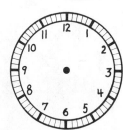

5. The time was →

Joe ran for
25 minutes.

Then the
time was ⟶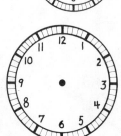

6. The time was →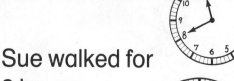

Sue walked for
2 hours.

Then the
time was ⟶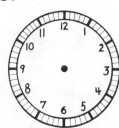

Birthdays Are Fun!

Write the name of your birthday month on the calendar.
Write the numbers for the days of that month this year.

			_____			
Sunday	Monday	Tuesday	Wednesday	Thursday	Friday	Saturday

1. In what month were you born? _____

2. In what month were you one month old? _____

3. In what month were you six months old? _____

4. How many months after your birthday is Halloween? ___

5. How many months after your birthday is Thanksgiving?

_____

6. How many months before your birthday is July 4th? ___

7. What is your favorite month? Tell why. _____

Name _____

Pet Litters

A litter is the number of baby animals born at one time. Look at the chart. Answer the questions below. Write number sentences to show your answers.

	Guinea pig	Goat	Rabbit	Hedgehog
Number in a litter	2 to 6	1 to 3	10 to 15	3 to 7

1. Which animal has the biggest difference between its

   smallest litter and its largest? _____

   ____ ◯ ____ ▢ ____

2. Which animal has the smallest difference between its

   smallest litter and its largest? _____

   ____ ◯ ____ ▢ ____

3. If a guinea pig, goat, and hedgehog had litters at the same time, what is the greatest number of babies they

   could have? ____ ◯ ____ ◯ ____ ▢ ____

4. What is the difference between a rabbit's largest litter

   and a hedgehog's largest litter? ____ ◯ ____ ▢ ____

Name _____

Buy It

How could you pay?

Use your coin punchouts to help you decide.
Use the fewest coins possible.

	Dimes	Nickels	Pennies
27¢	2	1	2
35¢			
16¢			
9¢			
56¢			
44¢			

Name _____

What Coins Are In the Banks?

Look at the amount. Look at the number of coins.

1.
12¢ 3 coins

_2_ pennies ___ nickels

_1_ dimes ___ quarters

2.
27¢ 3 coins

___ pennies ___ nickels

___ dimes ___ quarters

3.
15¢ 2 coins

___ pennies ___ nickels

___ dimes ___ quarters

4.
6¢ 2 coins

___ pennies ___ nickels

___ dimes ___ quarters

5.
16¢ 3 coins

___ pennies ___ nickels

___ dimes ___ quarters

6.
11¢ 2 coins

___ pennies ___ nickels

___ dimes ___ quarters

7.
30¢ 2 coins

___ pennies ___ nickels

___ dimes ___ quarters

8.
7¢ 3 coins

___ pennies ___ nickels

___ dimes ___ quarters

Name _____

Calculators Make Sense

Use your . Add 1 for a penny. Add 5 for a nickel. Add 10 for a dime. Add 25 for a quarter. Add 50 for a half dollar. Fill in the blanks.

1.

 + + + = _____ ¢

2.

 + + + = _____ ¢

3.

 + + + = _____ ¢

4.

 + + + = _____ ¢

How Much Change Is Due?

Write the amount.
Draw coins that look like this: ⓵¢ ⑤¢ ⑩¢

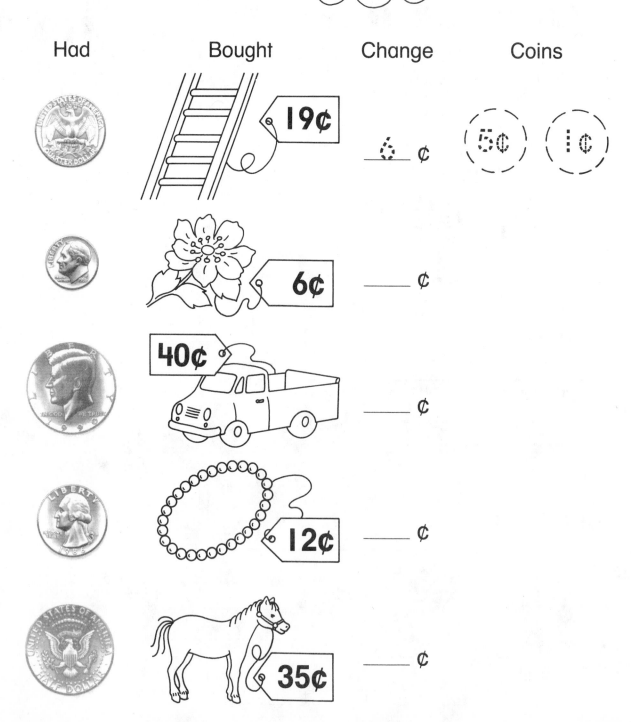

Had	Bought	Change	Coins
	19¢	6 ¢	5¢ 1¢
	6¢	___ ¢	
	40¢	___ ¢	
	12¢	___ ¢	
	35¢	___ ¢	

Round and Round You Go

Ride	Price
Carousel	20¢
Ferris Wheel	25¢
Bumper Cars	35¢
Roller Coaster	50¢
Loop-the-Loop	40¢
Parachute Jump	45¢
Moon Walk	15¢

Use the chart to answer the questions.

1. Maya likes the carousel best. She has 55¢. How do you think she will spend it? _____

_____

2. Karen earns 25¢ a day for helping at home. How many days will it take to earn enough for the moon walk,

carousel, and loop-the-loop? _____

3. Ricardo's little brother Juan loves the moon walk. The ride is 10 minutes long. How much money will Ricardo need to keep Juan on the moon walk ride for

30 minutes? _____

4. If you had 85¢, how would you spend it?

_____

Price Tag

Read each clue.
Write the answer on the price tag.

1. I am an odd number.
Count on 1, 2, or 3 pennies
from a quarter to find me.

2. I am an even number.
Count on 1, 2, or 3 pennies
from a dime to find me.

3. I am an odd number.
Count on 1, 2, or 3 pennies
from a nickel to find me.

4. I am an even number.
Count on 1, 2, or 3 pennies
from a half-dollar to find me.

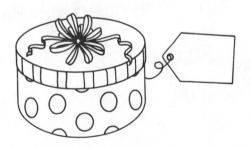

Balance the Scales

Which two numbers on
each side of the scale will
make the sums the same?
Write the sum in the △.

20/20   **10/30**

40

1.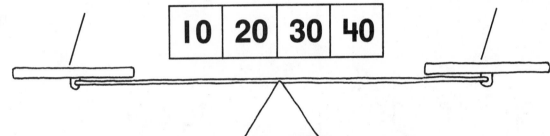

| 10 | 20 | 30 | 40 |

2.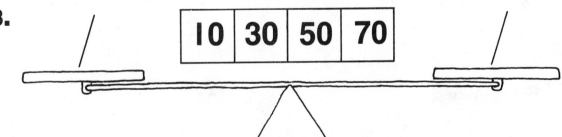

| 20 | 30 | 40 | 50 |

3.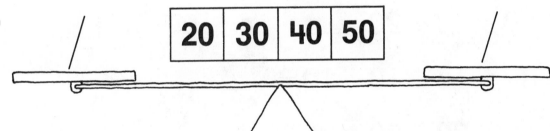

| 10 | 30 | 50 | 70 |

4.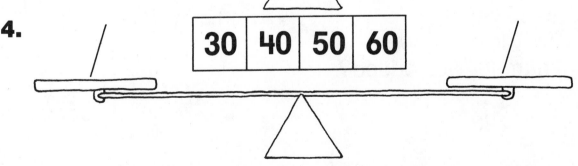

| 30 | 40 | 50 | 60 |

Using Your Head

Use mental math to find the sums.

1. Add 20 to each number.

    33 ____   67 ____

    24 ____   58 ____

2. Add 30 to each number.

    21 ____   16 ____

    52 ____   44 ____

Find the sums.

3. $23 + 10 + 10 =$ ____

4. $56 + 20 + 10 =$ ____

5. $20 + 28 + 20 =$ ____

6. $10 + 40 + 49 =$ ____

7. $30 + 17 + 10 + 10 =$ ____

8. $10 + 20 + 39 + 20 =$ ____

How old will you be?

9. in 10 years ____

10. in 20 years ____

11. in 30 years ____

12. in 50 years ____

What number was added?

13. $23 \rightarrow 43$ ____

14. $46 \rightarrow 86$ ____

15. $12 \rightarrow 62$ ____

16. $31 \rightarrow 91$ ____

Name _____

Shopping

16¢   13¢   9¢   27¢   24¢

Pick two things to buy.

Use punchout dimes and pennies to show the amounts.

Add to find the total cost.

Trade 10 pennies for 1 dime when you can.

Write the addition sentence and color the coins you will use.

1.

_____ + _____ = _____

2.

_____ + _____ = _____

3.

_____ + _____ = _____

4.

_____ + _____ = _____

Name _____

Party Problems

Look at the picture.
Write a number sentence to answer each question.

1. How many children are dressed as robots and monsters?

2. How many children did not dress as a ballerina?

3. How many rainbows and tulips are there?

4. How many more apples are there than children?

5. How many children are dressed in outfits no one else had chosen?

___ ○ ___ ○ ___ ○ ___ □ ___

Ladders Up

Use the numbers on each ladder to make the sum at the top of each house.

1.

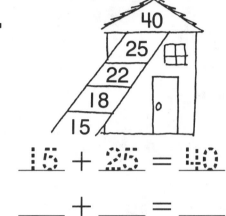

$\underline{15} + \underline{25} = \underline{40}$

___ + ___ = ___

2.

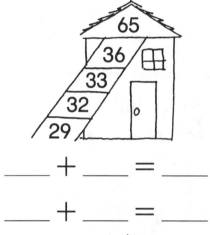

___ + ___ = ___

___ + ___ = ___

3.

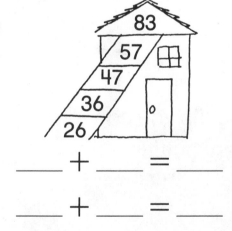

___ + ___ = ___

___ + ___ = ___

4.

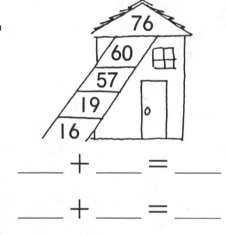

___ + ___ = ___

___ + ___ = ___

Write numbers on the ladder.
Then write addition sentences.

___ + ___ = 49

___ + ___ = 49

Name _____

Color Combinations

Use red, blue, brown, black, green, and yellow crayons.
Place the crayons in a bag.
Close your eyes and choose 1 crayon.
Open your eyes and color 1 piece of clothing.
Put that crayon aside.
Choose another crayon and color another
piece of clothing.
Do this 6 times in all.

Color to show how many different outfits you can make.
Hint: You may not need to color every outfit.

Name _____

Sports Club

The second and third graders have a sports club.
They form 2 teams to play each sport.

Sports Club					
	Monday	Tuesday	Wednesday	Thursday	Friday
Grade 2 members	10	5	8	13	10
Grade 3 members	12	6	10	10	14
1 baseball team = 9 players 1 basketball team = 5 players 1 soccer team = 11 players					

Use the chart to answer the questions.

1. On what days can the club play basketball?

_____

2. On what days can they play baseball?

_____

3. On what days can they play soccer?

_____

4. On what day do they have the right number of players

for exactly 2 soccer teams? _____

5. On what day do they have enough players for

exactly 2 baseball teams? _____

Using an Abacus to Add

This is an abacus.
The beads slide up and down.
To add on the abacus, slide a bead toward the middle bar.

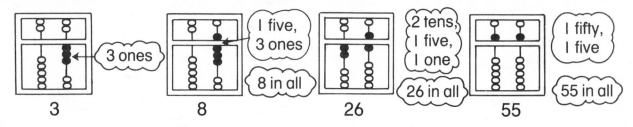

3 ones → 3

I five,
3 ones
8 in all → 8

2 tens,
I five,
I one
26 in all → 26

I fifty,
I five
55 in all → 55

Look at each abacus. Write the number. Find the sum.
Then draw beads to show the sum on the last abacus.

1.

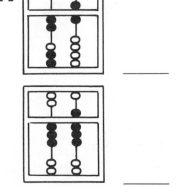 ____

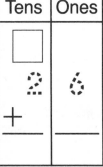

Tens	Ones
☐	
2	6
+	

____

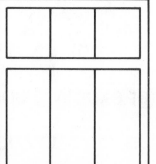

2.

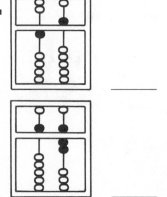 ____

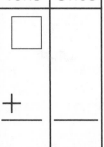

Tens	Ones
☐	
+	

Name _____

Catch the Match

Find a bat and a ball with Xs and Os that add
up to a number on a mitt.
Use 4 colors. Color each set of ball, bat, and
mitt a different color.

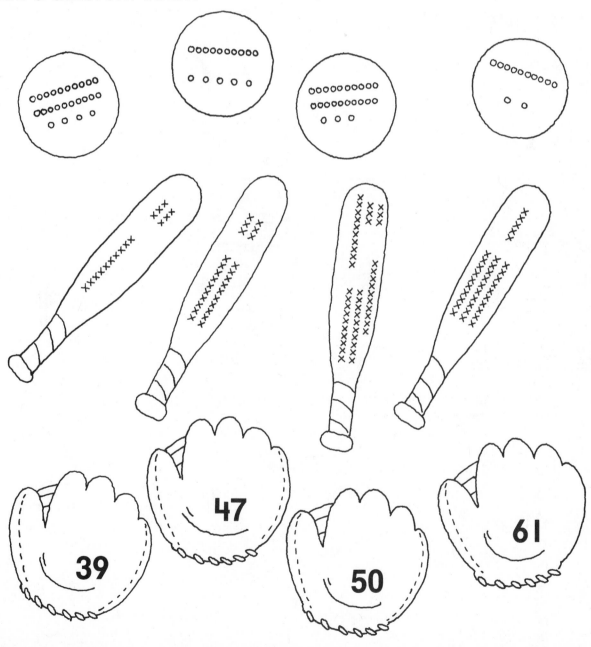

Math Mountain

Begin at **Start** at the bottom of the page.

Look at the four numbers that lead to each flag.

Decide which two numbers make the sum on the flag.

Ring those numbers. If you traded, color the flag.

Keep going up the mountain until you reach the top.

How many flags did you color? _____

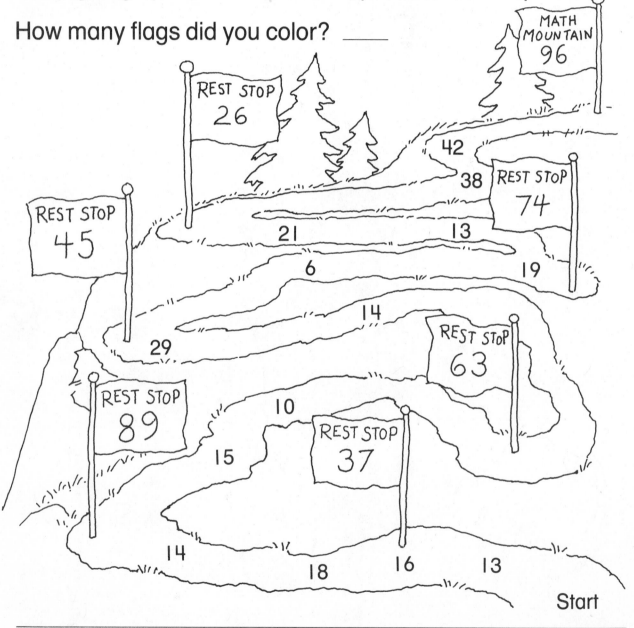

Name _____

Reading a Graph

The graph shows how much clay was used by each grade in one year. Analyze the graph to answer the questions.

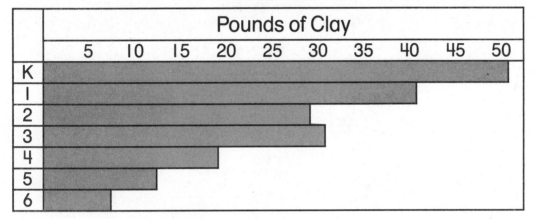

1. Which grade used about 50 pounds of clay? _____

2. Which grades used about 30 pounds each? _____

3. Which grade used about 40 pounds of clay? _____

4. Which grade used about 15 pounds of clay? _____

5. If the art teacher had only 60 pounds of clay, would that be enough for grades K and 1? _____

Use estimation to explain. _____

_____

_____

6. Which two grades could share 60 pounds of clay?

_____

Number Card Shuffle

Use the numbers on the cards.
Write problems that have the given answers.

1.

```
  5  2           □  □           □  □           □  □
+ 3  7         + □  □         + □  □         + □  □
─────────      ─────────      ─────────      ─────────
  8  9           8  0           9  8           6  2
```

2.

```
  □  □           □  □           □  □           □  □
+ □  □         + □  □         + □  □         + □  □
─────────      ─────────      ─────────      ─────────
  8  7           9  6           5  1           6  9
```

Write Your Own

Write your own addition question.
Then solve it and write the answer.

1.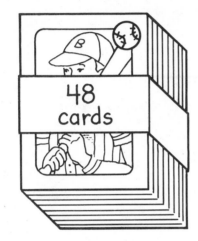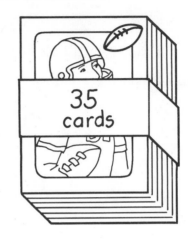

_____

_____

_____

_____

_____

_____   _____ cards

2.

Grade 2
Miss Kelly's class: 27 students
Mr. Brown's class: 24 students

_____

_____

_____

_____

_____

_____   _____ students

Match Up

Use mental math.

Color pairs of tags that add up to $1.00 (100¢) the same color.

Use a different color for each pair.

Check using paper and pencil or a calculator.

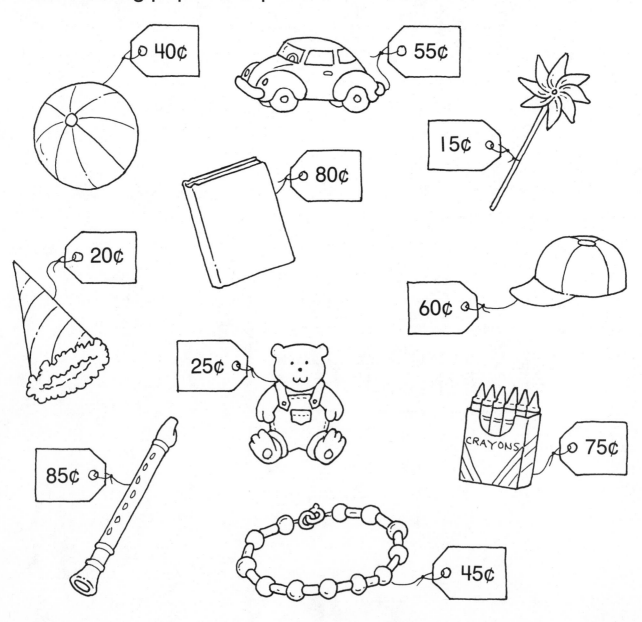

Name _____

Cards, Children, and Miles

Write your own addition problem. Then solve.

1.

$$\begin{array}{r} 11 \\ 38 \\ +46 \\ \hline \end{array}$$ How many cards in all?

_____

_____

_____

_____ cards
answer

2.

Attendance Report
Miss Ray's class: 24 children
Mr. Kelly's class: 27 children
Mrs. Brown's class: 25 children

_____

_____

_____

_____ children
answer

3.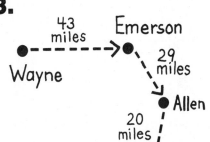

43 miles — Emerson
Wayne 29 miles
Allen
20 miles
Wakefield

_____

_____

_____

_____ miles
answer

Buying Trip

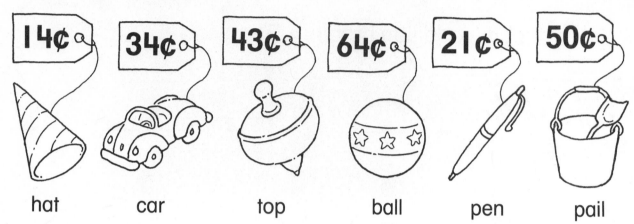

| hat | car | top | ball | pen | pail |

Estimate to help you find what each person bought.
Write the names of the items on the lines.

1. Nancy spent about 50¢. She bought 2 things.
   Nancy did not buy a car. What did she buy?

   _____

2. José spent about 90¢. He bought 3 things.
   One of the things was a top. What did José buy?

   _____

3. Sara spent about 80¢. She bought 3 things.
   She did not buy a top. What did Sara buy?

   _____

4. Josh spent more than 1 dollar. He bought
   2 of the same thing. What did Josh buy?

   _____

Solids at Home

Dear Family,
    In our math class we are learning to identify solid figures and match them to real-world objects. Help your child match solids to objects around the house and complete the chart.

Look around your house.
Find objects with the same shape as the solids on the chart.
Ask a family member to help you write the names of the objects to finish the chart.

rectangular prism	sphere	cylinder	cube	cone

Name _____

Sort the Solids

 1
sphere

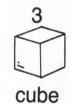 2
cone

 3
cube

 4
pyramid

 5
triangular
prism

 6
cylinder

 7
rectangular
prism

Read each sentence. Write the number of each solid
that matches.

1. It rolls.

_____

2. You can stack one on
top of another.

_____

3. It always has a square
face.

_____

4. It has faces of
different shapes.

_____

5. It rolls and slides.

_____

6. It has more corners
than faces.

_____

Name _____

Picture This

Find the plane figures in each picture.

What solid could you use to draw it?

Color a space on the graph each time the solid figure could be used to make a picture.

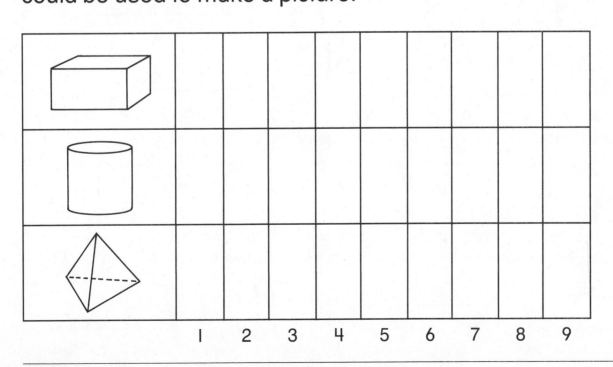

	1	2	3	4	5	6	7	8	9

TS-2   Use with text pages 253–254.   **105**

Make a New Shape

Put two closed shapes together to make a new shape.
Make the new shape on the geoboard. Write the number
of sides and corners.

1.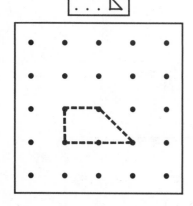

sides _____

corners _____

2.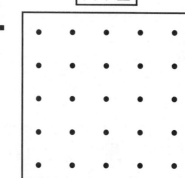

sides _____

corners _____

3.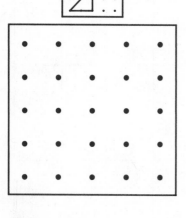

sides _____

corners _____

4.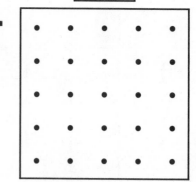

sides _____

corners _____

Name _____

Turns of the Board

Make each figure on your geoboard.
Think about how many times you will have to turn the board
for it to look like the second picture.   Ring your guess.
Then check and ring your answer.

	Guess	Check

1.

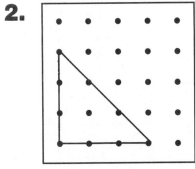 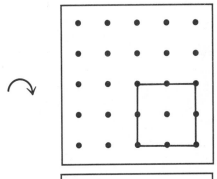

Guess: I 2 3   Check: I 2 3

2.

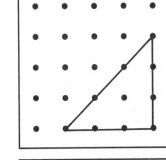

Guess: I 2 3   Check: I 2 3

3.

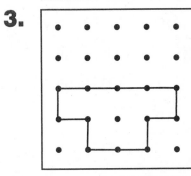 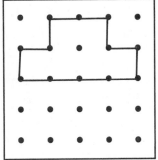

Guess: I 2 3   Check: I 2 3

4.

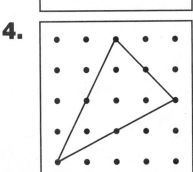 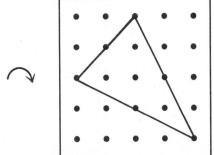

Guess: I 2 3   Check: I 2 3

Name _____

Fun with Folds

The figures below can be folded in more than one way
so that both halves match exactly. Show how.
Draw the lines of symmetry.

1.

2.

3.

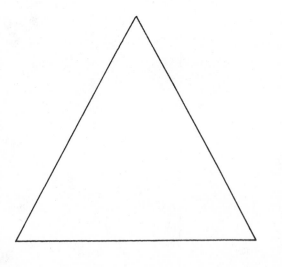

4. Draw a figure of your
own that can be folded
into matching halves.

Make My Shape

Work with a partner.
Each of you needs a work page.
Take turns connecting dots to make a figure.
Ask your partner to make the same figure.
Check to make sure your figures are congruent.

1.

2.

3.

4.

How Much?

Use skip counting to solve. Make a table if you need to.

1. Lisa wants to buy 5 stickers. Each one costs 2¢. How much does Lisa need?

____

2. The rides at the fair cost 3¢ each. How much would it cost for 4 rides.?

____

3. Kareem earns 5¢ a day for setting the table. How much will he earn after 5 days?

____

4. Roger bought 7 marbles. Each one cost 2¢. How much did Roger spend?

____

5. Yung-Su wants to mail 4 letters. Each letter needs a 10¢ stamp. How much will Yung-Su have to pay for the stamps?

____

6. At Sally's Sewing Store buttons come in packs of 2 for 5¢. How much would it cost for 8 buttons?

____

Collecting

1. Adam, Betty, and Carlo collect stamps.
Adam has 42 stamps.
Betty has 4 less than Carlo.
Carlo has 3 less than Adam.
Draw a line between each box of stamps and the
person who owns it.

Adam

Betty

Carlo

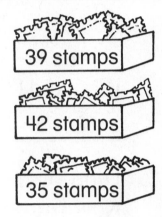
39 stamps

42 stamps

35 stamps

2. Diane, Eddie, and Fran collect postcards.
Fran has 5 less than Diane.
Eddie has 2 less than Fran.
Diane has 38 postcards in her collection.
Draw a line between each box of postcards and the
person who owns it.

Diane

Eddie

Fran

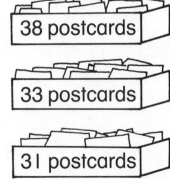
38 postcards

33 postcards

31 postcards

Name _____

What Did I Buy?

Use your coin punchouts.
Match each story to the toy that was bought.

1. I had 50¢.
Now I have

.

What did I buy?

_____

2. I had 90¢.
Now I have

.

What did I buy?

_____

3. I had 90¢.
Now I have

.

What did I buy?

_____

4. I had 70¢.
Now I have

.

What did I buy?

_____

Tens Count Back

Write the answers in the blanks.

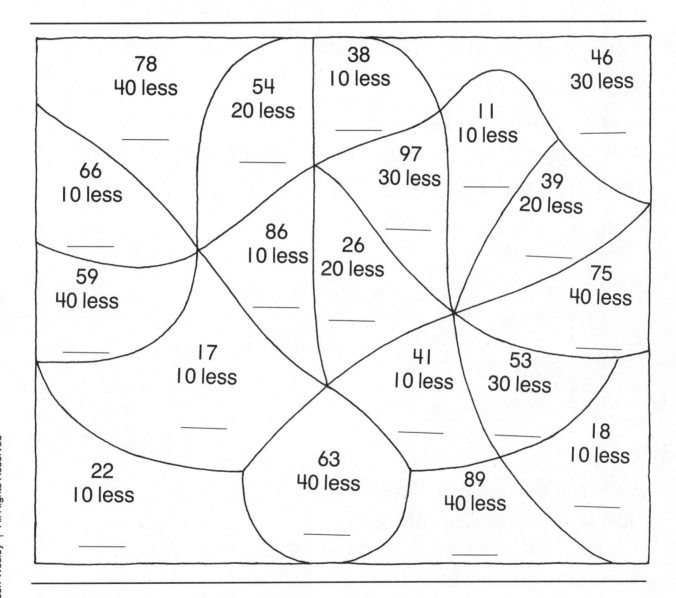

Find these answers above:

34   28   76   67   6   7   23   31   23

Color the spaces yellow. What does the picture show?

_____

How Many Ways?

Get 30 cubes.
How many different ways do you think there are to separate the cubes into 2 groups?

Write your guess here. _____
Separate the cubes into 2 equal groups.
Add 1 to the first group and take away 1 from the second group each time. Write the numbers.

15 and **15**	____ and ____	____ and ____
16 and **14**	____ and ____	____ and ____
____ and ____	____ and ____	____ and ____
____ and ____	____ and ____	____ and ____
____ and ____	____ and ____	____ and ____

How many ways are there? ____
How close was your guess?
What do you notice about the number of ways and the number in each group at the start?

_____
- -
_____

Try one on your own. Use an even number of cubes.
(An even number ends in 0, 2, 4, 6, or 8.)

Chicken Pox!

There are 39 students in the second grade.
Each day more students stayed home with chicken pox.
Look at the chart.
How many students stayed home each day?
Write the number sentence and your answer for each
day in the chart.

	Students at School	Number Sentence	Students with Chicken Pox
Mon.	28	39 – 28 = 11	11
Tues.	25		
Wed.	22		
Thurs.	19		
Fri.	16		

What pattern do you notice in the answers?

_____

- -

_____

Name _____

Break Apart a Ten?

Imagine you have the cubes shown.
Ring the amounts you could take away without breaking apart a ten.
Use cubes to check.

1.

3   9   4   7

2.

8   16   21   12

3.

26   12   31   23

4.

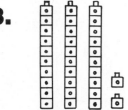

15   17   29   24

5.

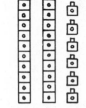

28   35   41   13

Pet Problems

Liane takes care of all the pets on Park Street.

<u>First</u> she walks a dog named Gus. He lives in the 5th house on the street.

<u>Next</u> she feeds a cat named Snow. Snow lives next to Sam.

<u>Then</u> she cleans Elsa's birdcage. Elsa lives between the fish and Gus.

<u>After that</u> she feeds the fish, Harry and Hilda. They live in the middle house on the street.

<u>Finally</u> she cleans the aquarium for a turtle named Sam. He lives in the 2nd house on the street.

Draw 5 ⌂ .

Use the clues to write the name of the animal that lives in each house. Then number the houses to show the order Liane follows when she cares for the pets.

Begin ●———————   Park Street   ———————→ ● End

Name _____

Trading

Finish the table.

Before the Trade		After the Trade	
Number	Tens and Ones	Tens and Ones	Number
52	5 tens 2 ones	4 tens 12 ones	4 12 / 5 2
65	6 tens 5 ones	___ tens ___ ones	
83	___ tens ___ ones	___ tens ___ ones	
	4 tens 6 ones	___ tens ___ ones	3 16
	___ tens ___ ones	___ tens ___ ones	6 18 / 7 8
	___ tens ___ ones	5 tens 12 ones	5 12

Name _____

Where Do They Go?

Use the numbers in the sun.
Put them in the boxes below.
Use each number one time.
Use your base-ten blocks to help.

1.

Tens	Ones
1	7
−	9
	☐

Tens	Ones
1	5
−	☐
	8

Tens	Ones
1	1
−	☐
	7

Tens	Ones
☐	☐
−	9
1	9

2.

Tens	Ones
2	2
−	9
☐	☐

Tens	Ones
2	7
−	☐
1	8

Tens	Ones
1	3
−	☐
1	1

Tens	Ones
☐	☐
−	7
	4

3.

Tens	Ones
3	2
−	7
☐	☐

Tens	Ones
6	1
−☐	☐
4	9

Tens	Ones
4	3
−☐	☐
3	3

Tens	Ones
☐	☐
− 1	1
1	9

Name _____

Weigh In

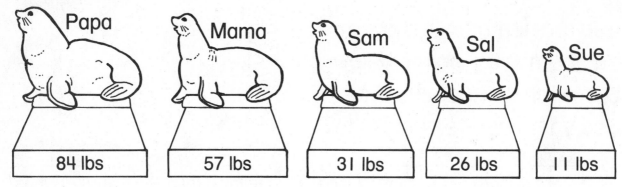

Papa — 84 lbs Mama — 57 lbs Sam — 31 lbs Sal — 26 lbs Sue — 11 lbs

Use the weights of the Seal family to answer the questions.

1. How much more does Sal weigh than Sue? _____

2. How many pounds would Sue have to gain to weigh the

   same as Sam? _____

3. How much would Mama Seal weigh if she lost

   35 pounds? _____

4. Which two seals together weigh the same as

   Mama Seal? _____

5. How much would Sam weigh if he lost 5 pounds?

   _____

6. Which seal weighs about 30 pounds less than

   Mama Seal? _____

7. How much less does Mama Seal weigh than

   Papa Seal? _____

Follow the Arrows

Count back in your head to subtract. Follow the arrows.

1. ⇨ means subtract 5.

2. ⇨ means subtract 10.

3. ➡ means subtract 2, ⇨ means subtract 10.

4. ➡ means subtract 10, ⇨ means subtract 5.

5. ⇨ means subtract 20, ➡ means subtract 4.

Name _____

Make a Difference!

Ring the two numbers whose difference is close to the number given.

1. 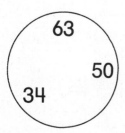   about 20

2. 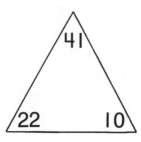   about 10

3. 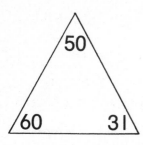   about 30

4. 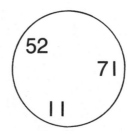   about 40

5. 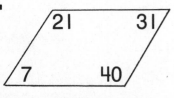   about 15

6. 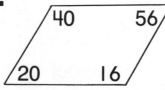   about 25

7. 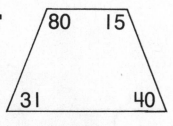   about 50

8. 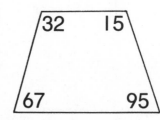   about 60

Magic Squares

Dear Family,
   Your child has been learning how to add to check subtraction. Work with your child on these addition-subtraction boxes to develop this skill.

Finish each box by subtracting and adding.
Subtract and add in the directions shown by the arrows.
Then check.   The first one has been done for you.

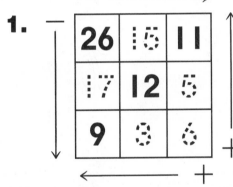

1.

26	15	11
17	12	5
9	3	6

2.

42	11	
20		9

3.

	30	35
30		15

4.

79		
		4
54	32	

5.

	48	
53	32	
39		

6. Try your own!

Answers:

2.

42	11	31
20	11	9
22	0	22

3.

65	30	35
30	15	15
35	15	20

4.

79	53	26
25	21	4
54	32	22

5.

92	48	44
53	32	21
39	16	23

Play Ball!

Kim, Jim, and Tim need new sports equipment.
Read the clues to find out what each one will buy.
Write the answer in the sentence.
Then find out how much more money each one needs.

Jim: It has a wood handle.
I use it to hit a ball.
I play with 1 or 3
other people on a court.
I have $28.

I need ____ to buy the _____ .

Tim: It has a wood handle.
I use it to hit a ball.
I play on a team.
We play on a field. I have $19.

I need ____ to buy the _____ .

Kim: It has a wood handle.
I play on a team.
We play on ice. I have $18.

I need ____ to buy the _____ .

$24

$56

$9

$32

Name _____

Predicting Patterns

Find the pattern. Write what happens to the difference.

1.
$$\begin{array}{r} 76 \\ -58 \\ \hline \end{array}$$
$$\begin{array}{r} 77 \\ -58 \\ \hline \end{array}$$
$$\begin{array}{r} 78 \\ -58 \\ \hline \end{array}$$
$$\begin{array}{r} 79 \\ -58 \\ \hline \end{array}$$
$$\begin{array}{r} 80 \\ -58 \\ \hline \end{array}$$

2.
$$\begin{array}{r} 52 \\ -16 \\ \hline \end{array}$$
$$\begin{array}{r} 52 \\ -18 \\ \hline \end{array}$$
$$\begin{array}{r} 52 \\ -20 \\ \hline \end{array}$$
$$\begin{array}{r} 52 \\ -22 \\ \hline \end{array}$$
$$\begin{array}{r} 52 \\ -24 \\ \hline \end{array}$$

3.
$$\begin{array}{r} 71 \\ -12 \\ \hline \end{array}$$
$$\begin{array}{r} 72 \\ -13 \\ \hline \end{array}$$
$$\begin{array}{r} 73 \\ -14 \\ \hline \end{array}$$
$$\begin{array}{r} 74 \\ -15 \\ \hline \end{array}$$
$$\begin{array}{r} 75 \\ -16 \\ \hline \end{array}$$

4.
$$\begin{array}{r} 48 \\ -23 \\ \hline \end{array}$$
$$\begin{array}{r} 58 \\ -23 \\ \hline \end{array}$$
$$\begin{array}{r} 68 \\ -23 \\ \hline \end{array}$$
$$\begin{array}{r} 78 \\ -23 \\ \hline \end{array}$$
$$\begin{array}{r} 88 \\ -23 \\ \hline \end{array}$$

Summer Rentals

Draw a line to show what each person can rent.
Use mental math to solve.

Name _____

Sums and Differences

Use these numbers to write 6 addition and 6 subtraction problems. Make each problem different.

| 48 | 23 | 56 | 17 |

1.   + ____

2.   + ____

3.   + ____

4.   + ____

5.   − ____

6.   − ____

7.   + ____

8.   + ____

9.   − ____

10.   − ____

11.   − ____

12.   − ____

Name _____

3 Winners

The winners of 3 different races compared their times.

Sack Race Team

3-Legged Team

Wheelbarrow Team

Read the clues in the chart.

Write the time each winning team took to finish.

Ring the fastest team.

Sack Race Team	3-Legged Team	Wheelbarrow Team
Our time is an odd number of minutes. It is greater than 20, but less than 30. One digit is a 5.	Our time is an even number of minutes. The number is more than 20 and less than 25. We ran 3 minutes faster than the sack race team.	We finished in an even number of minutes. It is more than 20. One digit is a 3. We ran 8 minutes slower than the 3-legged team.
Time: ____ minutes	Time: ____ minutes	Time: ____ minutes

Part Puzzlers

Draw lines to show equal parts.

1.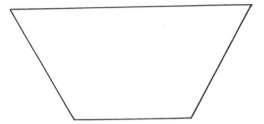

3 equal parts

2.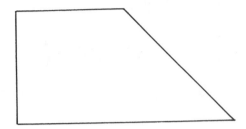

3 equal parts

3.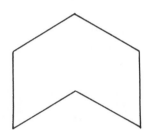

2 equal parts

4.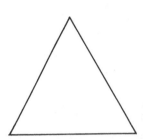

4 equal parts

5.

5 equal parts

6.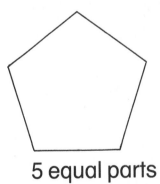

5 equal parts

7.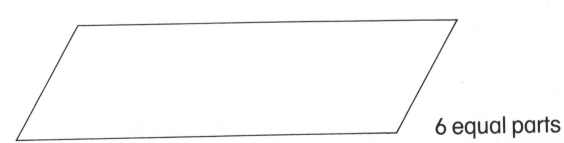

6 equal parts

Name _____

Pattern Block Fractions

Use pattern blocks.
Ring the correct word or words in each sentence.

1. Two red blocks cover the (orange, yellow) block.

2. Two (green, tan) blocks cover the blue block.

3. Three (green, blue) blocks cover the (yellow, orange) block.

4. (Five, Six) green blocks cover the (red, yellow) block.

Cover part of the shape with pattern blocks.
Trace and color to match.
Write the fraction for the colored part.

1. Cover 1 half.

 ____

2. Cover 2 thirds.

 ____

3. Cover 1 third.

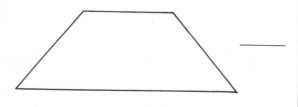 ____

4. Cover 3 sixths.

 ____

Fraction Match

Match the figures that show the same fractions.
Write the fraction next to the second figure.

1. 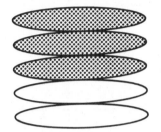    → [ ]

2. 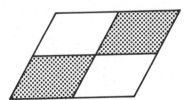   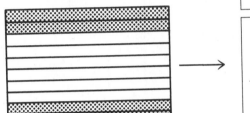 → [ ]

3. 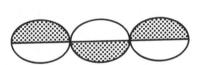   → [ ]

4. 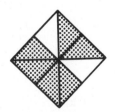   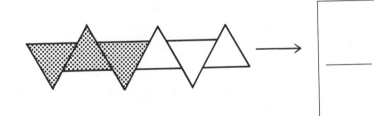 → [ ]

5. 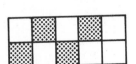   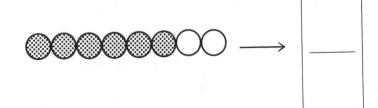 → [ ]

Name _____

Robot Fractions

Draw smiles on two sixths of the robots.
Draw sad faces on two sixths of the robots.
Draw freckles on one sixth of the robots.
Put hats on three sixths of the robots.
Draw ears on two sixths of the robots.

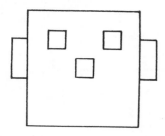
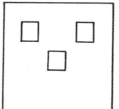
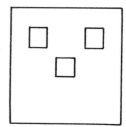

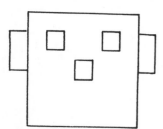
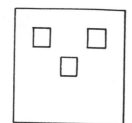

Now answer the questions about the robots.

1. What fraction of the robots still need a mouth? _____

2. What fraction of the robots do not have hats? _____

3. What fraction of the robots do not have freckles? _____

4. What fraction of the robots have ears now? _____

Recipe Fun

Jan asked 2 friends to come over.
She wants to use this recipe to make a special drink.

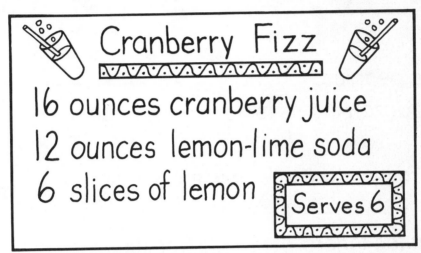

How much of each should Jan use to serve just 3?
Use counters to help. Write the answers.

_____ ounces of cranberry juice

_____ ounces of lemon-lime soda

_____ slices of lemon

Now write 3 number sentences to show what you did.

_____

_____

_____

Figuring Fractions

1.

Look at the pennies.
Write the fraction that tells how many heads. _____

Write the fraction that tells how many tails. _____

2. Look at the letters. Write the fractions.

A   N   S   I   E   K   T   X   O   C

Vowels: _____

Consonants: _____

Letters with only straight lines: _____

Letters with only curved lines: _____

3. Write numbers in the box to make these sentences true:

$\frac{3}{8}$ of the numbers are odd. $\frac{5}{8}$ of the numbers are even.

Name _____

More than One Whole

$$\frac{4}{4} = 1 \qquad\qquad 1\frac{1}{4}$$

(one whole)   (one and one-fourth)

Match.

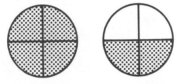

1. $1\frac{1}{2}$

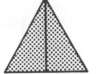

2. $1\frac{2}{3}$

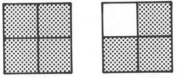

3. $1\frac{1}{3}$

4. $1\frac{2}{4}$

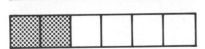

5. $1\frac{3}{4}$

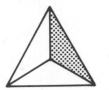

6. $1\frac{2}{6}$

Name _____

Show the Ways

Use counters.
Figure out which number in the box you can use to make the different equal groups.
Ring the number. Draw dots to show the ways.

1. 2 groups

3 groups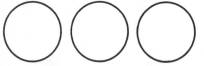

9	6
7	8

2. 3 groups

5 groups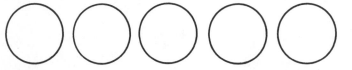

18	20
15	12

3. 2 groups

3 groups

12	16
18	20

4 groups

6 groups

Name _____

Nail the Boards

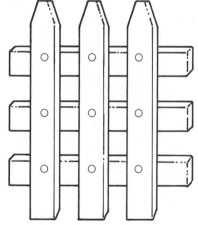

Draw a nail for each .
Then write a multiplication
sentence to show how many nails.

1.

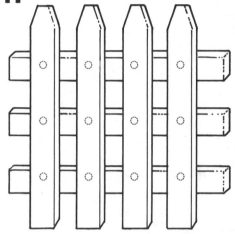

_3_ × _4_ = _12_

2.

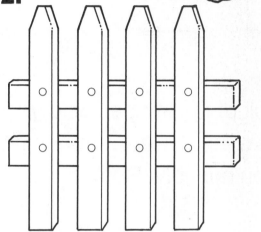

___ × ___ = ___

3.

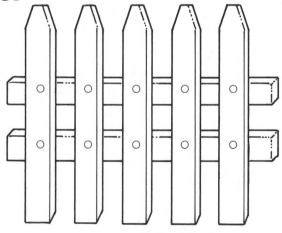

___ × ___ = ___

4.

___ × ___ = ___

Name _____

What Shape Is Your Money In?

Look at the shapes below.
Write the correct number in each shape.
Then multiply. Remember to write $ in the answer.

1.  2.

3.  4.

5. 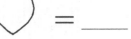 6.

7.  8.

9. Write your own shape multiplication sentence.

_____ × _____ = _____

Flower Power

Color the flowers. The arrow shows the direction of the rows.

1. Color red two rows of five flowers.
2. Color yellow four rows of three flowers.
3. Color pink two rows of three flowers.
4. Color purple five rows of two flowers.
5. Color orange three rows of four flowers.
6. Color blue three rows of two flowers.

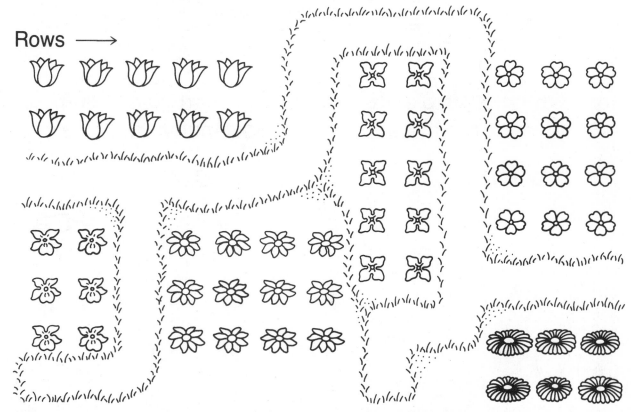

Rows ⟶

Match the color flowers that are turnarounds.

red   yellow   pink

orange   blue   purple

Two Operations in One

How many are there in all?
Use multiplication first. Then add.

1.

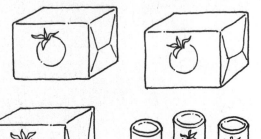

4 in each case, 3 extra
How many are there?

_____ cans

2.

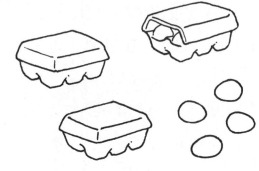

5 in each box, 4 extra
How many are there?

_____ eggs

3.

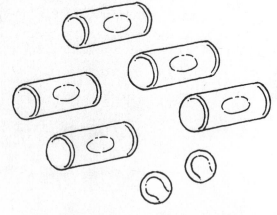

3 in each can, 2 extra
How many are there?

_____ tennis balls

4.

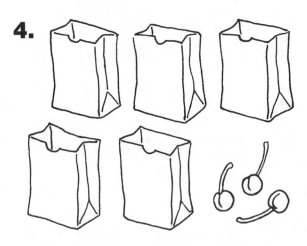

4 in each bag, 3 extra
How many are there?

_____ cherries

Name _____

School Trip

We are going to visit a farm!
Each car will hold 3 third graders
　　　　　OR 4 second graders
　　　　　OR 5 first graders.
Decide how many cars are needed.
Write the division sentence and draw the cars.

1. 15 first graders

need __3__ cars.

__15__ ÷ __5__ = __3__

2. 20 second graders

need ____ cars.

____ ÷ ____ = ____

3. 12 third graders

need ____ cars.

____ ÷ ____ = ____

4. 20 first graders

need ____ cars.

____ ÷ ____ = ____

Name _____

She Sells Seashells by the Seashore

Sheila sells her shells by the bag.
How much does each shell cost?
Write the division sentence.

A

___ ÷ ___ = ___ ¢

B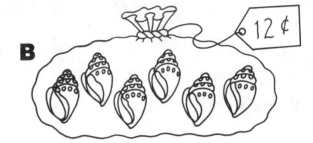

___ ÷ ___ = ___ ¢

C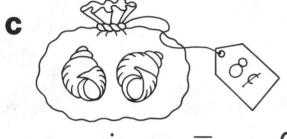

___ ÷ ___ = ___ ¢

D

___ ÷ ___ = ___ ¢

E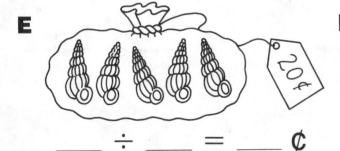

___ ÷ ___ = ___ ¢

F

___ ÷ ___ = ___ ¢

Compare the cost of each of the shells.

1. Which shells cost the least money? _____

2. Which shells cost the most money? _____

3. Which shells cost the same amount? _____

Related Facts

Dear Family,
   Your child is learning about the relationship between multiplication and division. Help your child fill in the multiplication tables below. Then together name the related division fact for each multiplication fact.

Some Related Multiplication and Division Facts

× 2	1		3		5
	2	4		8	

$2 \times 5 = 10$

$10 \div 5 = 2$

× 3	1	2		4	
	3		9	12	

$3 \times 4 = 12$

$12 \div 4 = 3$

× 4	1		3	4	
	4	8			20

$4 \times 2 = 8$

$8 \div 2 = 4$

× 5	1	2			5
	5		15	20	

$5 \times 1 = 5$

$5 \div 1 = 5$

Name _____

Drinks for Sale

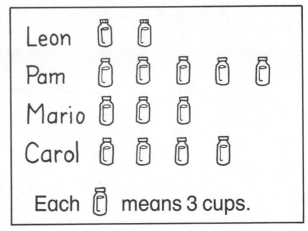

Lemonade Sold

Leon	🍶 🍶
Pam	🍶 🍶 🍶 🍶
Mario	🍶 🍶 🍶 🍶 🍶
Carol	🍶 🍶 🍶

Each 🍶 means 4 cups.

Apple Cider Sold

Leon	🍾 🍾
Pam	🍾 🍾 🍾 🍾 🍾
Mario	🍾 🍾 🍾
Carol	🍾 🍾 🍾 🍾

Each 🍾 means 3 cups.

Use another piece of paper to solve.
Ring the answers.

1. Who sold 16 cups of lemonade?   Pam   Mario

2. Who sold 9 cups of cider?   Mario   Carol

3. Did Leon sell more cups
   of lemonade or cider?   cider   lemonade

4. Who sold the same number
   of cups of lemonade and cider?   Pam   Carol

5. How many more cups of
   lemonade did Mario sell
   than Leon?   12   8

6. How many more cups of
   lemonade did Mario sell
   than cider?   8   11

Name _____

Number Models

Imagine that you have only these blocks.
Cross out the numbers you could not model.

124	255	~~169~~	301	533
222	140	238	492	721
406	244	136	373	175
321	650	154	312	480
837	181	453	509	382

Name _____

Mystery Numbers

Read the clues. Ring the number.

1. It has 7 hundreds.
It has 6 ones.

572	677
728	756

2. It has 6 tens.
It has 2 ones.

364	462
672	586

3. It has 4 hundreds.
It does not have an 8.

426	482
428	327

4. It has more tens than hundreds.
It has more ones than tens.

857	532
288	369

5. It has all of these digits: 6, 2, and 9.
The 2 is in the ones place.

629	862
962	296

6. It has the same number of tens and ones.
It has fewer hundreds.

778	477
877	445

Name _____

Make a Number

Make number cards for $\boxed{3}$ $\boxed{8}$ $\boxed{4}$.
Move the cards around to make six 3-digit numbers.
Write the numbers.

_____   _____   _____

_____   _____   _____

Make a number card for $\boxed{6}$.
Move all 4 number cards around to make
more 3-digit numbers.
Write the new numbers.

_____   _____   _____

_____   _____   _____

_____   _____   _____

_____   _____   _____

Name _____

A-maze-ing Patterns

Follow the trails from the top of the chart to the bottom.
Use blue for the trail that counts by 1s.
Use red for the trail that counts by 10s.
Predict which path will end at the highest number.

Start   **Start**

378→379	150	165	125→135	467	381	382
215	380	389	388	168	145	139	351	383
175	390	381 blue	382	387	155 red	385	384	153
392	391	189	383	165	386	410	409	402
393	302	384	185	175	147	814	304	657
689	394	195	385	386	388	389	351	525
527	395	205	435	387	305	390	401	602
235	225	215	397	175	392	391	487	400
296	245	255	285	295	393	681	125	297
250	410	265	275	394	305	315	325	335
427	415	397	396	395	215	378	355	345
215	842	398	402	395	385	375	365	312
417	290	399	414	405	419	904	535	320
315	602	400	567	415	514	805	317	942

Which trail ends on the highest number? _____

Name _____

More or Less

Write the numbers.

10 less		10 more		10 less		10 more
1. _____,	568,	_____		_____,	229,	_____
2. _____,	335,	_____		_____,	841,	_____
3. _____,	482,	_____		_____,	753,	_____
4. _____,	694,	_____		_____,	176,	_____
5. _____,	717,	_____		_____,	103,	_____

100 less		100 more		100 less		100 more
6. _____,	269,	_____		_____,	481,	_____
7. _____,	735,	_____		_____,	122,	_____
8. _____,	812,	_____		_____,	358,	_____
9. _____,	550,	_____		_____,	235,	_____
10. _____,	310,	_____		_____,	401,	_____
11. _____,	606,	_____		_____,	188,	_____

Name _____

Think Fast

Count on or back by tens or hundreds to solve.
Write the answers.

1. 237 people were on the plane. 30 people got off in Kansas City. How many people were left on the plane?

_____ people

2. 186 people were on the plane. 20 more people got on in Denver. How many people were on the plane then?

_____ people

3. Two planes left for Miami. One plane had 345 people, the other had 300 people. How many people went to Miami in all?

_____ people

4. 550 people bought tickets to New York. 300 people bought tickets to Los Angeles. How many more people were going to New York?

_____ people

5. If a jet can travel 500 miles in one hour, how many miles can it travel in 2 hours?

_____ miles

6. From Boston it is 400 miles to Buffalo and 551 miles to Cleveland. How much farther is it to Cleveland?

_____ miles

Heavy Weights

Make number cards for these numbers.

| 501 | 296 | 345 | 766 | 947 | 623 |

Place a number card on each blank weight to make a true number sentence.

When you are sure all 6 sentences are true,

write the numbers on the weights.

1.

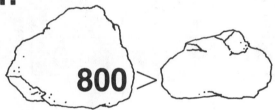

800 >

2.

< 950

3.

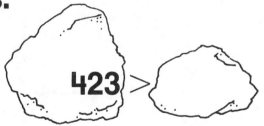

423 >

4.

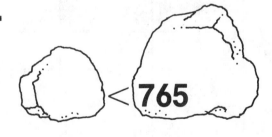

< 765

5.

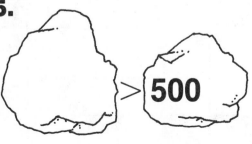

> 500

6.

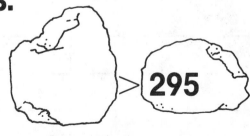

> 295

Name _____

Dollar Daze

Dear Family,
    Our class just learned to count dollars and cents. Watch as your child fills in the chart below. You may want to give your child real coins for help.

Tell ways you can make one dollar.
Complete the chart.

$1	50¢	25¢	10¢	5¢	1¢
1	0	0	0	0	0

Use with text pages 367 – 368.

Name _____

House Hunt

Al, Bob, Carla, and Diane live in these houses.

If Carla lives in a corner house,
and Bob lives next door to Al,
which ways are possible? Ring them.

A = Al
B = Bob
C = Carla
D = Diane

C, B, A, D   C, A, B, D   C, A, D, B

B, A, C, D   D, B, A, C   A, D, B, C

C, D, A, B   A, B, D, C   A, B, C, D

D, A, B, C   D, A, C, B   B, A, D, C

C, B, D, A   B, C, D, A   C, D, B, A

If Bob also lives next door to Carla,
and Carla lives in the last house,
which way is right? Write their names.

_____ , _____ , _____ , _____

Name _____

Hundreds of Things

Solve each problem. Ring the correct pictures.

1. Jack bought 600 seeds. He bought 2 packs. One pack had fewer than 200 seeds.

2. Sharon had 700 pennies. She had 3 banks.

3. Hector had 2 jars of beans. Each jar had more than 300 beans. He had 900 beans in all.

4. Val read 3 books. She read 800 pages. Two books had the same number of pages.

Graphic Details

The first, second, and third graders raised money for a community project. Each grade made greeting cards. They sold the cards at the winter and spring school fairs. The first grade sold 60 cards in the winter and 70 in the spring. The second grade sold 80 cards at each fair. The third grade sold 70 cards at the first fair and 40 cards at the second one.

Use the numbers in the story to fill in the graph.

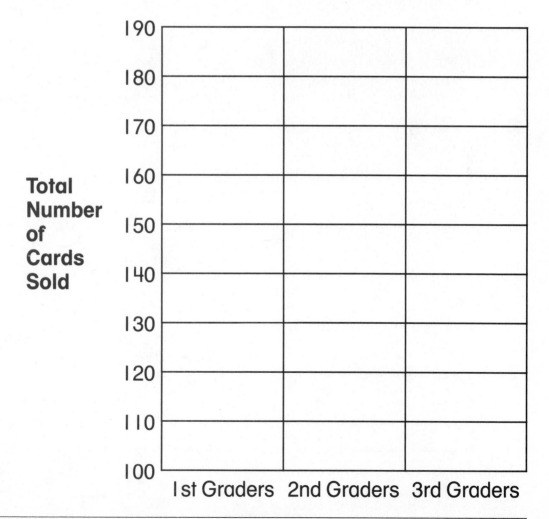

Name _____

What's the Missing Digit?

Write the missing digit in the box.

1.
```
  1 ☐ 3
+ 3 4 6
-------
  5 1 9
```
```
  3 2 3
+ 1 ☐ 1
-------
  5 0 4
```
```
  2 ☐ 2
+ 3 4 5
-------
  6 3 7
```

2.
```
  6 ☐ 2
+ 1 7 4
-------
  8 5 6
```
```
  3 9 7
+ 4 ☐ 0
-------
  8 2 7
```
```
  6 ☐ 5
+ 2 9 1
-------
  9 5 6
```

3.
```
  3 ☐ 2
+ 4 6 6
-------
  8 2 8
```
```
  1 2 7
+ 3 ☐ 1
-------
  5 1 8
```
```
  5 ☐ 1
+ 2 9 8
-------
  8 7 9
```

Bake Sale

Nicole kept a tally of the goods sold at the bake sale.

1. Color the bar graph to show the data.

Use the graph to answer the questions.

2. How many more cookies were sold than muffins?

_____ more cookies

3. How many fewer pieces of pie were sold than rolls?

_____ fewer pieces of pie

4. How many baked goods were sold in all?

_____ baked goods

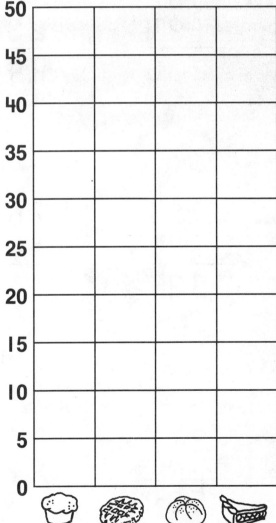

Baked Goods Sold

Name _____

Grading Janet's Paper

Put an X on each incorrect answer.
Correct each problem Janet missed.

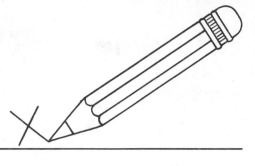

Name ___Janet___

1.
$$
\begin{array}{r} 362 \\ -124 \\ \hline 238 \end{array}
\qquad
\begin{array}{r} 686 \\ -238 \\ \hline 448 \end{array}
\qquad
\begin{array}{r} 574 \\ -127 \\ \hline 453 \end{array}
\qquad
\begin{array}{r} 645 \\ -135 \\ \hline 510 \end{array}
$$

2.
$$
\begin{array}{r} 951 \\ -125 \\ \hline 827 \end{array}
\qquad
\begin{array}{r} 760 \\ -602 \\ \hline 158 \end{array}
\qquad
\begin{array}{r} 482 \\ -\ 49 \\ \hline 433 \end{array}
\qquad
\begin{array}{r} 853 \\ -218 \\ \hline 634 \end{array}
$$

3.
$$
\begin{array}{r} 894 \\ -335 \\ \hline 559 \end{array}
\qquad
\begin{array}{r} 683 \\ -655 \\ \hline 32 \end{array}
\qquad
\begin{array}{r} 745 \\ -123 \\ \hline 612 \end{array}
\qquad
\begin{array}{r} 570 \\ -139 \\ \hline 431 \end{array}
$$

Name _____

Fruit Vote

The students voted for their favorite fruits. Apples were chosen by 140 students, oranges by 190 students, and bananas by 210 students. Draw the correct number of apples, oranges, and bananas on the graph. Each piece of fruit stands for 10 votes.

= 10 votes   = 10 votes   = 10 votes

Favorite Fruits at Montclair School

140 apples	
190 oranges	
210 bananas	

Use the graph to answer the questions.

1. What fruit did the most students choose? _____

2. What was the second favorite? _____

3. How many more students chose bananas than chose apples? _____

4. How many more students chose bananas than chose oranges? _____

Name _____

Walking to School

Read the story.

Anita, Wendy, Juan, and Joaquin live on Park Lane. Wendy walks 315 steps to get to school. She lives the farthest away from school. Anita lives next to Wendy. Anita is 35 steps closer to school than Wendy. Juan lives between Joaquin and Anita. Juan lives 160 steps closer to school than Wendy. Joaquin walks 72 steps to get to Juan's house.

Write **Anita, Wendy, Juan,** or **Joaquin** to identify each child's house.

How many steps does each child walk to school?
Show your work to prove your answer.

Wendy	Anita	Juan	Joaquin
	☐☐	☐☐	☐☐
____ steps	____ steps	____ steps	____ steps

Name _____

Reading a Menu

Menu			
Bean soup	$1.50	Green Salad	$2.00
Noodle soup	$1.70	Chicken salad	$2.50
		Shrimp salad	$3.00

1. Jean had soup and salad. She spent $4.50. What did she have?

_____

_____

2. Bill had soup and salad. He spent $3.50. What did he have?

_____

_____

3. Patty had soup and salad. The salad was $1.00 more than the soup. What did she have?

_____

_____

4. Ted had soup and salad. The salad was $1.30 more than the soup. What did he have?

_____

_____

5. Sue and Jerry each had a bowl of soup. They spent $3.00 in all. What did they have?

_____

_____

6. Joe had two different salads. He spent $5.00. What did he have?

_____

_____

Name _____

Time Tables

Solve. Make tables to help.

1. Belinda picked 2 baskets of berries in the morning and 3 baskets of berries in the afternoon. Each basket had 30 berries. How many berries did she pick in all?

_____ berries

2. Neil can pack 15 boxes in 2 hours. How long will it take him to pack 75 boxes?

_____ hours

3. Carey does 20 sit-ups each day. How many sit-ups does he do in one week?

_____ sit-ups

4. Anna can walk a mile in 20 minutes. How many miles can she walk in 1 hour?

_____ miles

5. Jody spends $2 a month on soap and $1 a month on toothpaste. How much does she spend on soap and toothpaste in 1 year?

_____

6. A play was performed each day from Monday through Friday. Each day the auditorium was full. The auditorium holds 150 people. How many people saw the play?

_____ people